WIRDS AN 'E SEASONS ROON

on an
Aberdeenshire Farm

Alexander Fenton, CBE

Drawings by
Colin Hendry, FSA Scot.

THE MERCAT PRESS
EDINBURGH

First published 1987 by Aberdeen University Press
Reprinted 1992 by Mercat Press at James Thin
53–59 South Bridge, Edinburgh EH1 1YS
© Alexander Fenton 1987, 1992
© Illustrations — Colin Hendry 1987, 1992

All rights reserved. No part of this publication may be reproduced, stored in a retrieval system or transmitted in any form or by any means, electronic, mechanical, photocopying, recording or otherwise without prior permission in writing of the publishers.

ISBN 1873644167

Printed in Great Britain by BPCC–AUP Aberdeen Ltd.

CONTENTS

Italicised words will be found in the Glossary. Unusual words in quoted speech, though not italicised, are also glossed.

LIST OF ILLUSTRATIONS

Photographs   All photographs are from colour transparencies taken by the author.

Drawings   Drawings have been re-done by Colin Hendry, FSA Scot, of the Science, Technology and Working Life Department, National Museums of Scotland, from original rough sketches by the author.

PREFACE

This book is about the seasonal round on a small Aberdeenshire farm looked at through the words and expressions and tools, equipment and techniques that were the farmers' stock-in-trade in and around the parish of Auchterless. Though the knowledge of one farmer on one farm is taken as a base, this was part of a common pool of knowledge for a wide surrounding area. This is nevertheless a localised study. People from 50 or 100 miles away will be able to identify differences in pronunciations and vocabulary.

The period covered is roughly the second quarter of the twentieth century. The farmer was the late James Hunter, of Brownhill in the parish of Auchterless, born at Tollo Croft in 1887. The family entered the farm of Brownhill in 1922. I absorbed much information from James Hunter in the course of many years of talking and working with him in the fields and about the houses, and in the late 1950s and early 1960s the information was entered systematically into notebooks. In addition, use has been made of farm diaries running from 1923 till the late 1960s. Farm diaries with such quality of detail are unusual. By placing notes and diaries together, a good picture appears of the rhythm of the farming year, and of a farmer's attitude to his working world.

The details of words and work that have been discussed still lie within living memory. Much more could have been said, but what follows is enough to show how much can be recorded from oral sources, supplemented by diaries and any other writing and by direct observation, about a period that is already astonishingly remote.

Using the 1938 *Diary* as a sample, it appears that, when related tasks are grouped together, tillage and preparation of the soil amounted to 101 days or 27.7 per cent of the working year; the sowing and harvesting of cereals to 80 days or 22 per cent; the planting and gathering of root crops (including dunging and weeding) to 93 days or 25.5 per cent; and hay or grass to 20 days or 5.5 per cent. This is a typical Buchan farming pattern, clearly demonstrating the emphasis on cattle, for which Northeast Scotland is famous.

The period covered by this book shaped the character of the North East as we know it. The more we learn about that period, the more we will understand our background and the more we will appreciate the tremendous distance we have travelled so quickly in more recent times. Publications like the *Scottish National Dictionary* and the *Concise Scots Dictionary* preserve the words we have used and still use, and should continue to use. Museums like the Northeast Agricultural Heritage Centre at Aden Country Park, and the National Museums of Scotland's Scottish Agricultural Museum in the Royal Highland Showground at Ingliston, provide displays of the tools and equipment of those days and teach young and old what they meant to our immediate ancestors.

Wirds an' Wark 'e Seasons Roon tries to go a little further, by combining words and things, and looking at words and things through the voices and hands of the people who lived and worked then. It is a tribute to the farmers who made Buchan. I am grateful that I was brought up amongst them.

THE BEGINNING

The new year begins with the last stroke of the clock as December fades into January. By then, young and old have already been making preparations of various kinds, and it is with these that the round of the new season really begins.

In the early evening, not so many years ago, the *guisers* came to the door, with soot-blackened faces and schoolbags to hold the good things they hoped to get. They knocked at the doors and recited, more or less in harmony:

> Rise up aal' wife an' shak yer feathers
> Dinna think 'at we are beggars,
> We're only bairnies come tae play,
> Rise up an gie's wir Hogmanay.

1   Guizers at Brownhill in 1958.

Wir feet's caal, wir sheen's thin
Gie's a piece an' let's rin.

Yer purse is fu' o' sillar,
Yer bottle's fu' o' beer
Ye'll surely gie's a baabee
Tae spen' 'e neesht New 'Ear.

They were invited in, girls were chaffed about 'lads' and boys were chaffed about 'blon'es', they were pressed to sing and might do so, bashfully, after much persuasion. At last they got an apple, an orange, a slice of cold dumpling, a penny or a threepenny bit, and ran off to finish their round before going home to hang up their stockings, and dream of what they might find there in the morning. Stockings were hung up on New Year's Eve and not at Christmas amongst the Presbyterian population of Auchterless and the parishes around.

In general, work went on as usual on the last day of the year, ploughing or thrashing, or taking a trip to the town to catch up on unpaid bills for boot

2   The march-fence between Brownhill and Curriedown.

repairs or farm tools. Older farmers sometimes liked to reminisce, on the subjects dearest to their hearts:

We have had lots of storm through the end of year and rough gales and rain it has been a slow job lots of stopages with the ploughing we had a wonderful harvest got the stuff in very fine condition. Sales has been stoped for a long time Foot and Mouth disease and like to be a new case in papers today (*Diary*, 31 December 1923).

The first of January was taken as a day off, with a good 'New 'Ear's denner' and visits paid by and to friends. The essential work in byre and stable and the feeding of poultry went on as usual.

On the second, however, celebrations were over and work went on as normal.

THE FORCE

The manpower at Brownhill consisted in the early days of James Hunter senior, his son Jim (from whom much of this information was recorded) and a *fee't man*, with temporary additional help each year.

The man who *bailied* (looked after the cattle) first when the family moved to Brownhill was Willie Laing, nicknamed 'Groatie Laing' because 'he spak a lot aboot a groat' (a coin). He had two *kists* with him in the *chaamer*, 'een for eez siller an' een for eez claes'. He used a gas-tin in the *chaamer* for his water, till a man persuaded a boy to bore holes in the bottom of it. As the 1923 *Diary* tells, 'a man Laing came up at dinner time engaged to come here till Whitsunday' (27 March), 'a man Laing came home forenoon to start work' (2 April). He was said to have been there for the 'winter half 'ear', but the *Diary* shows that his stay was for two months only.

Willie Beddie or 'Beedie' came at the May term in 1923 and stayed for over thirty years, earning a long-service medal from the Royal Highland and Agricultural Society. Mr Hunter was not too well in one of the first summers, and a man called Geordie Sim was *fee'd* to work the horse. He was someone they had known before, since he had paid occasional visits: 'Geo. Sim was over evening' (3 September 1923). He was 'a hivvy kinna lad, puffin' an' blaain' a bittie. The forks 'at ca'd aff 'e shaves on 'e binder, they were gaan roon an' roon an' 'e craaled in anaith 'er tae see fit wis wrang. "There's nae muckle", said he, "that I dinna ken aboot a binder." He couldna mak oot fit was wrang so hid a look 'imsel' an' saa at eence 'at 'e check spring was broken.'

Willie Beddie had only one *kist*. This was normal in *chaamers*, though *bothy* lads would have two, one for clothes and one for food. There was no *bothyin'* in this area, however, and the *fee'd* men living in the *chaamer* got their meals in the farm-kitchen. They did not have to prepare food themselves.

Willie used a *chackie*, a kind of cloth bag like a pillowcase, originally made of checked cloth, for carrying his dirty washing to the lady up the road who did his washing for him. The bag was closed by a long tape that went round his shoulders for easy carrying on the bicycle, the open end of the tape being tied round a marble or small object put in the bottom corner of the bag as a

4

3 Willie Beddie (second from left) getting his long-service medal in the 1960s.

retaining device. The use of *chackies* goes very much with the coming of bicycles. Before that a kind of *portmanty*, a bag with a hand-grip, was carried, not very convenient for cycling with.

There was a *caff-bed* in the *chaamer*, on which Willie always slept, the chaff being replaced at the time of a threshing.

Before he came to Brownhill, Willie had, like all farm-servants, moved around from farm to farm. He had been at Feithhill with John Morrison, at Mains o' Tollo with George Minty, at the Denmoss, at Easter Aucharney and several more, gaining a geat deal of experience of the kind and nature of the farms within a circuit of ten or a dozen miles. Single men often moved every six months, and married *cottar-men* once a year. 'There wis some claase—jist an unwritten laa—that if the fairmer didna seek them tae bide, they hid tae go.' They would describe themselves as 'nae socht'. On the other hand, they might say, 'I got a blast 'e day', meaning that the farmer had asked them to stay—'bit 'em 'at didna get a blast, their name wis Walker'.

Willie married the daughter of Jimmy Shirran at Pitglassie Smiddy, and had been staying there about the time of the Porter Fair feeing market. 'He wis tellt tae cry in aboot Broonhill, an' 'e wis jist fixed up.' He always went to the Turriff and Huntly Feeing Markets as holidays. 'He wis aafa interestit in faa wis bidin' an' faa wis leavin' an' faar aabody wis gyaan.' He was a small man with 'a queer kin' o' wheeber o' a fustle', best heard when, for example, he was lying on top of a cart load of corn being led back to the cornyard.

'Some place he wis fee't up 'e Huntly wye, piz-meal wis rale common for 'e supper files. Oh, well, 'e fairmer he got his ben in 'e room, an' 'e dother widda been makkin' 'em in 'e kitchen. The fairmer he wid cry, "Fess ben my pizzers, Mary Anne Mann." Aye, Mann wis 'eir name, ye ken.'

On this relatively small farm, Willie was *bailie*, looking after the cattle, and the farmer was horseman, always the superior job. At places where there was a bigger force, there were also the *halflin* or *orra-loon*, the odd-job boy or 'apprentice' farm-servant, or the *strapper* or *shalt-loon*, the boy whose job was to look after the *shalt*. At week-ends, the man whose turn it was to be at home to look after the beasts was the *toondie* or *catcher*. Expressions were, 'Are ee toondie 'e day?', 'I'm catchin' 'e morn'.

There was a saying for small places with little more manpower than one: 'Big loon, little loon, grieve an' a', i.e. jack of all trades. There was no *grieve*, or farm overseer, as such, at Brownhill.

Also on the labour force was 'a deem in 'e hoose', Jessie Reid. She was also expected to do some outside work, including helping at threshing and at harvest work: 'Jessie and me pulled some sweeds and filled up 2 pits potatoes duke york and arran chief' (16 March 1923), 'Jess an me breaking dung we broke 16 drills' (6 June 1923).

At busy seasons, help was got from *quarterers*, some of whom came regularly for years. They were people with no fixed home, who took up their quarters in byre or stable for the period of work, or for a passing visit, before moving on. Neighbours came to help also. In 1929, for example, the entries were:

12 Feb	'John Reid our harvest man and another man with him a painter, got a bed in stable for the night.'
22 June	'We got in a stack morning last one Willie Merson, the boy Gray and John Reid was all assisting.'
24 July	'John Reid our old harvester came in about tonight.'
25 July	'John Reid left morning to Inverurie.'
29 Aug	'Alick Gray was here for the first day of harvest.'
30 Aug	'Mr Gray and boy here today.'
10 Sept	'John Reid harvest man came about dinner time.'

John Reid worked for 30 days and was paid £6. 5*s*. Alick Gray, from the Hill of Hatton, worked for 40 days and got £8. 6*s*. 8*d*. These, however, were the main extras in the course of the year. John Reid, and another *quarterer* called Gillan, were valued not only for the work they did but also for the entertainment they provided. Each had a good fund of stories.

Mr Hunter's grandfather used to 'fee hairsters aboot Cornhill at a kinno a market for 'e hairsters, 'e Berry Market o' Cornhill. Fin 'e cam hame, his wife said till 'im, "Hae ye gotten onybody?" "Aye", he says, "'e Lang Laddie an' 'e Blue Flee." "Oh", she says, "'at wis aafa names." "Oh", he says, "ye canna get gentlemen tae work yer work." Anither time 'e fee't an umman hairster an' fin she cam hame she hid on *skiry* kinno claes. 'Ey were badderin 'er aboot 'er claes, an' she said, "I'm nae prood. I'm tasty an' airy."'

The rest of the force consisted of the horses. There were three horses, and a *shalt* was kept earlier on, and used to pull the gig that was at one time kept in the gig-shed, and a sledge in the winter. It was also used for the light job of *shimmin' neeps*, and occasionally for pulling a light, granite roller. Horses were bought either at the fortnightly sales in Aberdeen, or sometimes at a *roup*: for example, a mare, Lady, was got at John and Billy Hunter's roup at Seggat. They were shod at Pitglassie Smiddy or at Fortrie Smiddy after the one at Pitglassie went out of use.

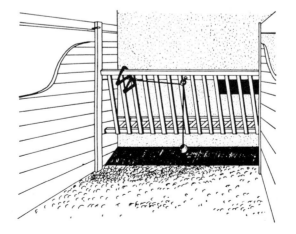

4   A *staa* in the stable, with a *sinker*.

The stable, alongside the gig-shed and next the *neep-shed*, had four *staa's* separated by three *trevises*. There were never more than three occupied, because the *shalt* was kept in the well creosoted wooden 'black shed'. The empty stall was used as a store for straw and hay.

For fastening in the stall, a *helter* went over the horse's face. The strap of it that went over the head was the *heid-stall*, and the bit behind the throat was the *throat-lash*. A rope of fair thickness ran from the halter and through a ring on the *forestaa*. To keep the rope from being pulled out, Mr Hunter would take the end of the rope round his hand with fingers outstretched and loop this into a knot big enough not to come through the ring. *Sinkers* of lignum vitae were used to keep the rope from coming through the ring. They were heavy so as to discourage the horse from 'haalin up an' doon its heid'; for the same reason, ropes were preferred to chains, which would have made a great noise if the horse indulged in this action.

In the corner under the window stood the *corn-kist* on which farm-servants were fond of sitting and singing their *cornkisters* or 'bothy ballads', beating time on the side with their boots. It was filled with the *bruise* from the corn loft, and in it lay a square wooden container, the *lippie*, used to

5   The *corn-kist* in the stable.

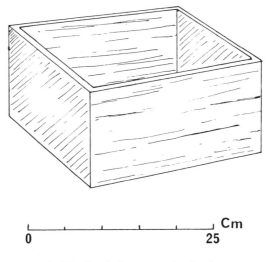

6　The *lippie* for measuring bruise.

measure out a feed of bruise. A horse got a 'lippiefae o' bruise' three times a day, or rather less when it was not working. As often as not, the *corn-kist* was referred to as the *bruise-box*.

The carting-harness was kept here: the bridles, the collars and *haims*, the *saiddles*, the leather *belly-ban's* with two or three chain links at each end, the *back-cheyn*, the *britchin*, and the *hin'-slings* which were either sewn or screwed on the bridle. There was an open type of bridle and a *blin' bridle*, which was fitted with blinkers. Bridles were for working only, but wooden *branks* could be used for leading the horse, for example when taking them out to grass, or in from it.

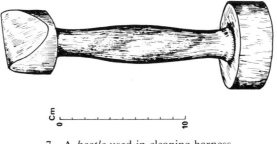

7　A *beetle* used in cleaning harness.

Harness was mostly bought at *roups*, so it went the rounds of the farms. Repairs were done by the saddler in Turriff. Against the back wall of the stable was a folding-down table used for polishing harness, in preparation for shows.

On the roofing couples there was a number of prize tickets, mainly of the Turriff District Agricultural Association: 'Highly Commended', or 'Very Highly Commended'.

Though a David Brown tractor was bought in the late 1940s, horses were not done away with at once. A black mare, Jip, was kept on as an old-age pensioner for light jobs like *shimmin* and sowing turnips, until she died in 1964.

8   A folding-down table in the stable, where harness was cleaned.

MILK, BUTTER AN' CHEESE

The work of the women, in and around the house and kitchen, in byre and milkhouse, and among the poultry, is completely ignored as a general rule in farmers' diaries, and Brownhill was no exception. Nevertheless, it went on all the year round, and underlies the details of milk and milk products, now to be given.

Milking was done in the byre, using a milk pail and a wooden *milkin'-steel*. Milk flowed from all four *tits* on the cow's *ether*, except when one was not working as a result of an illness such as mastitis, in which case this was the *blin' tit*. From the byre the pails of milk were carried to the *milk-hoose* at the end of the farm-house, there to be *syed* through a *sye, syer* or *milk-search* before being set in the milk dishes on the cool shelves. When the cream had risen, it was removed with a shallow metal pan, the *skimmer*, and put in the earthenware cream crock, the *ream pig*, till enough had accumulated for churning into butter. The cream would have soured a little first.

The older churns were upright and churning was done by means of a plunger, the handle of which moved up and down through an opening in the lid. The head was a circle of wood pierced by up to six round holes. This was the *plump-churn*, and the plunger could be called the *plumper*. The older word *kirn*, 'churn', both noun and verb, though well-known, had gone out of current spoken usage. The *plump-churn* was replaced by the table-churn with arms that rotated internally when a handle was turned, and by the much bigger barrel churn, the whole body of which turned end over end.

Whatever type of churn was used, it was *plottit* with boiling water before the cream was poured in. After churning for some time, the cream was *broken* and the particles began to *gaither* in a solid mass. It was then said, ''e butter's come'. Temperature was critical, however, and if the butter did not come readily, a cupful of boiling water was added.

The liquid buttermilk was drained off through the tap at the bottom of the table- or barrel-churn, or poured out at the top of the plump churn by tipping it, and was generally given to the hens. The butter itself was washed in the churn with cold water, which was drained off, and then washed a second time with cold water to which a 'han'fae o' saat' had been added.

9 A *plump-churn* with its plunger.

10 Whey flowing from a barrel churn.

11 Pounds of butter, with *clappers*.

The butter was lifted out, its fresh clean aroma spreading through the kitchen, and put into a *lame* milk-basin that had been *plottit* also. It was then made into rectangular blocks, 'pun's o' butter', by means of a pair of wooden *butter-clappers* with which the butter was squeezed and shaped. Different designs made of combinations of straight lines and diamond shapes were made on top with the edge of one of the *clappers*. The pounds of butter were for sale, or could be bartered at the grocer's van for other goods. For immediate domestic use, however, small balls called *pats* were made, enough to spread a slice of bread or a quarter of oatcakes.

Butter-making was a time of pleasure for young folk who were about, especially if there had been a recent baking of oatcakes (*cyacks* or *breid*), since they might get a *thoom' piece*, a piece of oatcake liberally spread with fresh butter scooped up and applied with the thumb.

Talk of butter not coming reminded Mr Hunter of some stories. 'There'd been queer things happenin' at ae time at Fowlie's croft at Easterfield, clods fleein' aboot, milk nae comin', an' 'at. They got 'e meenister in, bit naething happened fin he wis 'ere. It was a man Skerry fae 'e Moss o' Wartle 'at settled things at 'e eyn. He wis supposed tae hae dealt wi' 'e Deil.'

12   Mrs Brown making *pats* of butter.

Cheese was also made on the farm, though not in great quantities since the view was taken that it was better for the milk to go into the calves to give them a good start in life. It took a lot of milk to make cheese, both of the day's milkings or a little more. The extra amount added to make up the required quantity could be skimmed milk, but otherwise whole milk was used. It was *syed* into the pot, still warm from the cow, to remove cow hairs and other debris, and the pot was set over the fire to warm up. *Yirnin'* was added and the milk solidified. By the 1950s, the rennet came in bottles, though in earlier days a calf or a sheep's stomach was bought from the butcher, and cleaned and specially treated to coagulate the milk. The curd was broken, and the heat was increased till the *fye* rose to the top. Heating was done gently in a pot on the *bink* of the fire, away from the open flames.

The whey was poured off and the *crudes* were squeezed by hand till pliable. Salt was added and the curds were broken up completely by hand or

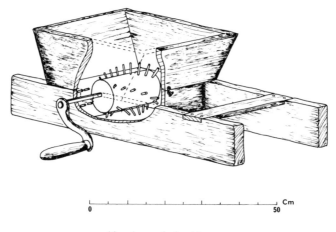

13   A *crude-brakker.*

were put through a wooden *crude-brakker* incorporating a handle-operated, spiked drum, or through an ordinary meat mincer. The broken and salted curds were then put into a wooden *chessel* or *chesset*, with holes in the side and base, which had previously been lined with wetted cheesecloth. It was packed to a level that left the lid protruding on top. The *chessel* was then put into a cheese press which at Brownhill was portable, and consisted of two substantial wooden planks joined by two steel screws. Many farms had heavy granite cheese presses. The screws were tightened every three of four days for about two weeks, till the surplus *fye* had been extruded through the *chessel* openings. The cylindrical cheese, the *kebbick* or *kibbick*, was then taken out, wrapped in muslin, and laid on a shelf in the gig-shed to continue to dry and mature.

If some *crudes* was left over from the amount needed for the *chessel*, it was put on a piece of cheese-cloth, twisted up tightly, and hung outside on the branch of a tree to dry. It was ready to eat, as a kind of soft cheese, in a day or two, with a fine, light skin around it and a wrinkled top where the folds of the cloth had been. This ball of cheese was called a *hangman* or *hangie* because it was hung up to dry.

Milk played a prominent role in other dishes. One, of milk alone, was *calfie's cheese*, made from the first (or more rarely the second) milk from a cow after calving. The milk was put in a dish and warmed in the oven till it became firm, with a skin on top, on which cinnamon could be sprinkled. This made a rich feast.

14   Filling the *chessel*.

15   The *chessel* goes into the press.

16   Cheeses drying in the gig-shed.

Much milk was also taken with the oatmeal dishes, *brose* and *pottitch*. *Brose* was a standard breakfast dish among farm folk, made of raw meal put into a wooden bowl, the *brose-caap*, and salt mixed in. Hard-boiling water was poured on, stirring being done the while with the handle of the spoon, which was then licked clean. Creamy milk from an earthenware bowl that was standing by was poured on top, and the *brose* was ready to be *suppit*. The milk left in the bowl was drunk to finish off.

(a)

(b)

(c)

17   (a) (b) (c) Stages in *brose*-making.

The main difference between *brose* and porridge was that the latter was boiled. It was reasonably standard practice in this district to eat porridge at supper-time, not for breakfast. Porridge could be made with milk as well as with water. Meal was sprinkled slowly by hand into the boiling liquid, stirring going on all the time, and the mixture allowed to *bile* again, with fairly frequent *steerin'* with a round wooden *spurkle* till it thickened properly, in about half an hour. It was said that in earlier times the porridge for the men's suppers was put on at the back of the fire at dinner-time and left to boil till supper-time so that the meal swelled enormously and went further. When ready, the porridge was poured into plates, and fresh meal sprinkled on top. It was supped by taking a spoonful of porridge and dipping this into the bowl of milk alongside. This milk was again drunk off at the end.

Another oatmeal dish, used for dinner, was *knotty tams*. The milk was boiled, and the meal was 'plumped' in quickly, in small *gowpenfaes* or handfuls, without stirring. It formed into lumps, of which the inside was only partially cooked, and was eaten with oatcakes.

A dish used instead of pudding at dinner, or sometimes as a supper dish, was *murly tuck*, occasionally also called *snap-an'-rattle*. The milk was heated till *loo-warm* and then a quarter of oatcakes was *murled* into it. The next job, according to the injunction, was to 'snap it up'!

Since some of the utensils used in milkhouses were bought from tinkers who came round the doors, it is appropriate to record two tinkers' sayings, one as reported by Mr Hunter, and the other by the housekeeper at Brownhill (who came originally from a neighbouring farm). Mr Hunter's version was:

> Will ye no buy a brander, a tander, a tilly-pan or a ladle? If ye'll no buy that ye'll no buy anything at all.

The housekeeper's version was much fuller, as befits the one who had most contact with the tinker:

> A roaster, a toaster, a brander, a strander, a wee bit jug for the bairn the day, good wife. If ye'll no buy that will ye no buy anything at aa? Could ye no gie's a wee bit butter the size o' a bum bee's knee tae the e'e.

BARN WARK

The periods covered by work in the barn were January to April and October to December, with a thresh or two in June and August to keep up the corn supplies.

The big sliding door of the barn opened on to the *cornyard*, so that sheaves could be forked in easily off the cart. Stacks were taken in and threshed weekly. The barn consisted of the *shafe-eyn* and the *strae-eyn* with the threshing mill between, and a *corn-laft* reached by a wooden stair. The sheaves, whose bands of straw or binder-twine were *lowsed* with a *lowsin' knife*, were fed into the mill at one end, the revolving drum beat out the grain, and the straw passed along the three *shakkers* of the mill to the *strae-eyn*, where any young lads about the place were given the job of 'trampin' 'e strae', to get as much packed in as possible. Beneath the *feedin' platform*, on which the man who was feeding the mill stood, was the *caff-hoose* where the loose chaff piled up. Hanging on a nail in the wall at the side of the *feedin' platform* was a *lowsin' knife*, made from the head of a walking stick, with a triangular section from a binder- or reaper-blade fixed in it to cut the bands

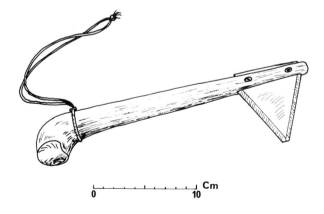

18   A home-made *lowsin'* knife.

19

of the sheaves. A loop of string at the top end was put round the wrist to make sure it was not dropped into the drum of the mill, which rotated so fast that it was dangerous if any solid object fell in. It dated to before 1922, for it was left at Brownhill by Sandy Mackinnon when he went out of the farm.

The threshing mill was made by 'William Alexander, Ribrae, Turriff, N.B., Millwright and Engineer' according to an oval wooden plate fixed on its side. The lettering is in red, outlined in black, on a gold background. It was driven be a paraffin engine made by the Aberdeen firm, Allan Brothers, dating back to 1909, and taken over at valuation in 1922.

The neighbouring farm of North Pitglassie was occupied by a relation through marriage, and the two places did a lot of *neeperin'*. A close eye was kept on the getting of a new mill and engine at North Pitglassie in 1923. The story comes from the *Diary* of that year, and the millwright was a relative, John Hunter:

3 Jan	'Wm. Merson down in the evening showing plans for Engine Stance.'
4 Jan	'over at Wartle afternoon seeing new mill—he has nearly finished.'
15 Jan	'Mr Merson's mill came here about 11 o'clock and motor lorry from Oldmeldrum, got on no so bad. We went up the grass feild the road was rather soft. We was up helping to take her off and put her in the barn. John busy afternoon making chaff house.'
17 Jan	'Wm Merson was down at Station (Turriff) for Engine and I was down with the millwright he had to look her over before he took delivery. We put her on in the evening and there was no exast pipe and we was like to be smothered with smoke.'
18 Jan	'We did not manage to get the Engine to go.'
19 Jan	'John came back this morning from Wartle with a crank to Engine. We had a stiff job and we sent over for Mennie the Blacksmith and we got a thrash in the afternoon, threshed fine. John away home again push bike.'
20 Jan	'I was down at Turriff . . . got pipe for Engine paid 2/-.'
17 Feb	Millwright and his father came over forenoon put up Elevators . . . Mill was on but the spout (for corn) was hardly acting right not much fall on it.'
20 Feb	'John the millwright was there and a motor fixing up the elevators.'
23 Feb	'I . . . went up past Segget telling Billie about the onset of Mr Merson's mill. He intends to come across tomorrow afternoon to see a thresh.'
24 Feb	'Mr Merson had a onset of his mill, Billie was over from Segget and Wm Hutcheon John and Alick from Wartle.'

And so, before witnesses, the new mill was well and truly launched, and the two months of excitement were over.

19   The *fanners* in the corn-loft, 1959.

The *corn-laft* was sited above the cart shed, so that heavy sacks could be dropped through a trap-door into the carts waiting below, or hoisted up from them. The side walls were smoothly plastered for cleanliness in working with the grain that ran up the elevators from the mill and dropped through the wooden spout onto the floor where it piled up in a golden heap. Alongside the pile was the *winnister*, *fan* or *fanners* by which the chaff and loose bits of straw were blown out of the corn. A large, two-handled scoop, the *backet*, was used to fill the *happer* of the fanners from the pile on the floor: 'Ye fullt 'e backet an' cowpit it intill 'e happer.' There were three *spoots* on the fanners. The one nearest the fan end was where the best quality grain, the good corn, came out. The spout at the far end was for 'secints' (seconds), grain of secondary quality used to feed the hens and the like. In between was a smaller spout for 'orra seeds'. This *winnister* was made by Shearer of Turriff. It was bought in 1929 at the Curriedown farm *roup* when the three Shands (Sandy, Willie and Rob) went out. The record appears in the *Diary* for that year:

22 May   'went over to sale at Curriedown bought two stirks a fan and a mangle and a horse power clipper and trocks (odds and ends).'

24 May   'I was over at Curriedown evening for the fan I bought at roup and went back for a handle I forgot.'

3 June   'we thrashed some we had in barn and took up the Curriedown fan to the loft and put the corn through. Weighed up 10 qrs. corn.'

Cleaned grain intended for sale was weighed up in the loft. For this, a *bussle* or *bushle* measure of oak was used, along with a cylindrical oaken *straik*, both of which had come from Carlincraig. In use, 'the bushle wis fullt raither mair than the bushle, an' 'e straik was grippit in baith han's, an' scooshled roon', nae rolled'. To get the weight of a bushel, the *straik* was taken across the top in this way, and bushel measure and contents were weighed together. The measure was then weighed empty, and the figure subtracted. The standard was 42 lb to a bushel, but in a good year the bushel might actually weigh 43-44 lb, when a bit more should be paid for the corn. In a bad year, it could fall to 37-38 lb, and was worth correspondingly less. Soft or damp corn gave poor weight.

A story was told of how a corn merchant went up to a corn loft and he and the farmer set about *straiking* a bushel to weigh it. As the merchant filled the grain into the measure out of a *backet*, the farmer tramped around on the wooden loft to make the vibration pack the corn better and give better weight, and so a better price.

Weighing was done on the *wyin-machine*, which had a green painted frame, and a red painted top and platform for holding the sacks. A cast metal plate on the side bore the name, 'Wm. Beaverly, Rothie'. It was an old one, bought at a roup in the Rothienorman district when Mr Hunter's grandfather was still at Carlincraig, between 1871 and 1887. It came to Brownhill from there in 1922. An old local name for a weighing machine, it was said, was *steilert* (steelyard).

The corn was usually weighed in ½ quarter bags, ie 168 lb or 4 bushels, whether the grain was for seed or for sale.

The corn-loft was used as a storage area also. There were balls and bunches of used binder-twine, waiting to be twisted with a ropetwister into three-strand ropes, for tying down thatch on the stacks. Such twisting was a wet weather job. One man sat with the twine on the floor of the barn, and the one with the twister moved back from him as the rope lengthened, going up the stair into the loft and then along it to get the length required. There was a wheeled *seck-barra* for moving full bags, and a hand-barrow described as a *seck-lifter*, because it was used for lifting sacks. Less sophisticated but

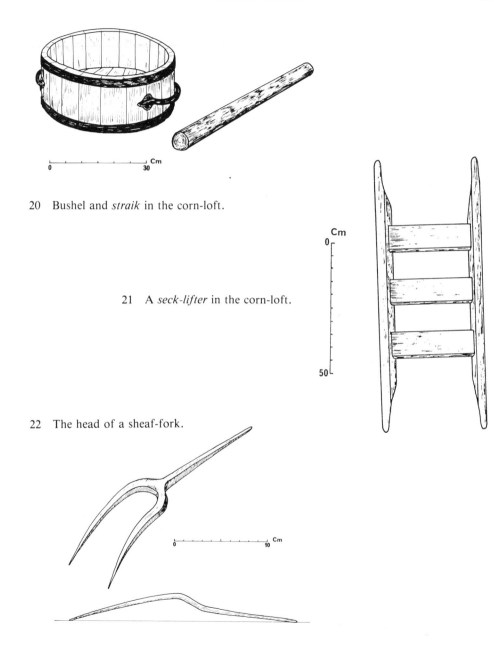

20   Bushel and *straik* in the corn-loft.

21   A *seck-lifter* in the corn-loft.

22   The head of a sheaf-fork.

equally effective was a short pole, perhaps a length of a broken shaft, used by two men when lifting a sack on to the back. The sack-barrow was made in 1929. The wood was supplied to G. Simpson, having been bought from Bruce the joiner in Turriff for 4s.3d., and the completed barrow was delivered on 17 May (*Diary, 1929*). A green-painted barrel with a lid was for storing hens' *mait*. Sacks of corn, potatoes and hens' food, and piles of empty sacks were on the floor. A wooden trestle with a flat top was used to hold reaper and binder blades when the sections were being sharpened; beside it were two binder blades and some binder canvasses. A round wooden riddle with a base of zinc perforated by 1/16 inch diameter holes was a *siftin' riddle*, used for cleaning turnip seed. There were two *blin' sieves* with bases of stretched calf-skin tacked on all round the wooden sides. These came from Carlincraig in 1922. When corn was being sown in a field with a *happer* slung to the front of the sower's chest, *blin' sieves* were used to carry corn from sacks to keep the *happer* filled. They were carried on the head, ready for easy tipping into the *happer*. An obsolete name for a *blin' sieve* was *wecht*.

The maker of the North Pitglassie mill, John Hunter at Wartle, had also made a *winnister* for George Merson. It was too stiff to drive, however, and somehow found its way into the Brownhill corn loft.

In one corner, above the drive from the engine, was the belt-operated cast-iron corn-bruiser, made by Harrison, McGregor & Co, Leigh, England (No. 5), with which *corn,* i.e. oats, was bruised to fill the *corn-kist* in the stable to feed the horses. It went out of use after horses were given up. It was taken over on valuation in 1922.

The wood-framed *backet* (scoop) with a metal base, for carrying and filling corn, was made by Jimmy Ogg in Turriff. He was a retired farm *grieve*, not a joiner to trade, but ''e files worked wi' Bruce 'e jiner'.

The *shafe-eyn* of the barn, constantly being refilled and emptied, had relatively little in it except a large barrel with a hinged half-lid that held feeding-stuffs for the hens, *ruck-covers* and one or two sheaf forks.

The *strae-eyn* was also fairly bare, though at the time of note-taking, the wooden *tummlin-tam*, hay-gatherer, was stored here.

There were more sheaf-forks, a four-toed fork stamped 'Berwick', and on a nail alongside the byre door, a four-toed *graip* made by C J Skelton & Co, Sheffield, along with a gin-trap for rats.

In Mr Hunter's time at Brownhill, straw was carried by forks or graips through to the byre, but there was an older custom, known to him though never used there. This was for the straw to be made into bunches called *winlins*, a common custom when the mill was water-driven and a little away from the rest of the houses, and where barn space was limited. The straw was gathered into bunches with the loose ends turned back and twisted round to make a compact mass that would not spill out straws as it was 'cairriet throwe 'e close'.

The *caff* from the *caff-hoose*, when it had piled up, was carried through to the byre to be used for bedding, not to waste it. The *beylie* was sometimes 'a bittie roch wi't' and would get a *caff* into one of the beast's eyes. He would try to snip it out with a handkerchief over one of his fingers. If this failed, he would grind some glass into a powder with a hammer, and blow it into the animal's eye with a little 'tubie', in the hope that the watering would do the trick. He had also tried sugar. As Mr Hunter said, 'I niver saa 'im get the caff oot o' a beast's e'e yet'. A *caff* in the eye was sore on the animals. A blue skin would grow over the eye, and it would water all the time. Its condition suffered.

The chaff also served a domestic purpose. Once a year, the *bowsters* in the beds were filled with fresh chaff, and for the first night or two afterwards the sleepers were in danger of rolling off, till the tightly packed chaff settled. This was a job done in May: 'filled up the chaff for the beds' on 4 May, and on 18 May, W Shand at Curriedown got four bags of chaff for a bed (*Diary 1929*).

Bigger farms had bigger *caff-hooses* where the ceremony of the 'horseman's word' was said to have been carried out. The *charge* that was taken was not unlike the Masonic oath.

Besides *caff*, there were also *cuffins*, short, broken bits of straw shaken out through the big holes of the *cuffin riddle* near the back end of the mill, underneath the shakers. A second riddle that formed part of the mill was the *siftin' riddle* that let small seeds through its zinc base, and a third was for *sheelicks*, small, light grains of corn that came out 'at a wee spootie' at the side of the mill. The kinds of seeds cleaned out through the *siftin' riddle* were of the weeds that were common amongst the corn: *knot girse*, *runch*, fat-hen or goosefoot ('it has a big kinno heid on't'), *yarr*, and *skellach*. There is often confusion between *runch* and *skelloch* in Buchan because of the similarity of the flowers. Other common weeds were *dockens* and *thristles*; and amongst the grass the yellow of *tansies* was a regular annual feature.

SPRING WARK

Ploughing and work in the barn took up much of the daylight time in January and February, and there were also regular tasks in byre and stable. As spring came, from March and on to May and June, the jobs diversified. April was one of the most intensive periods in the farming year, with the driving out of dung, grubbing and breaking in of ploughed land. The sowing of grain, grass-seed, turnip seed and artificial manures, harrowing and rolling, the opening of drills for potatoes and for turnips, *shimming* (horse hoeing) and gathering weeds, as well as other jobs like repairing fences before the beasts were let out to graze, took up all spare moments.

The driving of dung was done in box carts. In the field the *tail boord* was taken off and the dung pulled out into small heaps, regularly spaced through the field. The work of 'ca'in oot 'e midden' alternated with the surface spreading of the muck, using four-pronged *graips*.

The muck was of different qualities and purposes: 'driving out some short dung forenoon and put on new grass for hay', 'driving out . . . old short dung and put it on brae of new grass on shopie feild' (a field where there had once been a shop) (*Diary*, 19 and 21 January 1929). Once the midden was empty, the poultry house and ash pit were cleared. Part of the purpose of ploughing at this period, for example on stubble, was to turn the dung down into the soil. Horse dung from the stable was put on the brae where potatoes had been grown the year before.

By early March, the first spell of putting out and spreading muck was over, but artificials were being applied. In 1929, Porter's motor brought manure, and 16 cwt were sown on the *yavel* on 6 April. Eleven bags of manure were sown on the *neep* ground on 11 April, and given a *strake*, i.e. harrowed in. Two bags of potato manure were got from the Station on 8 May, and following this stage, the driving of dung began again, for potato drills were both dunged and manured. Dung was put on '12 drills and put over manure and potatoes and got dung broken', 'yocked carts and got a few drills dunged' (*Diary*, 10 and 16 May 1929). The driving and breaking of dung lasted till 1 June, and the sowing of manure till the 19th. The manure sowing machine, sometimes known as the *bone Davy* (from the earlier use of bone manure), was cleaned and laid past on the following day.

26

Preparation for the turnip and potato crops began in mid-March, with repairs to the grubber and drill-plough at the smiddy, but before they began to operate intensively the broadcast sowing machine was got out.

The folding halves of the *broadcast*, made by Ben Reid, Aberdeen, were kept in the corn-loft, and the less vulnerable, green-painted wheeled frame was kept in the cart-shed below. Two old plough-socks were attached to the frame. When sowing was in progress, they were fixed by chains, one at each end of the box, for use as markers. Latterly the horse-shafts were removed and stored in the straw-end of the barn, and the machine was adapted for use behind the tractor.

The *ley*, broken in with the grubber, was sown first and given a *strake* with the harrow. Grubbing was heavy work for which three-horses might be needed. A three-horse 'tree' (swingletree) for a grubber remains in the cartshed, though the grubber itself was sold to a scrap-merchant.

It was not regarded as good practice to use the farm's own seed too much so on the 'upwinding' and 'low winding' of the *park*, 5 quarters of corn from George Simpson, Danshillock, were sown, and only half a quarter of Brownhill's own (*Diary*, 25 March 1929). In spoken usage, the up- and low-

23   James Hunter sowing with a *happer*.

24   The broadcast sowing machine, adapted for use behind the David Brown
tractor, in 1962.

windings were the *eemist-* and *naithmist wynin's*. The four year old lea next
Curriedown was dealt with next, getting more of George Simpson's seed, and
on the afternoon of 27 March, they 'got most of it *thorthered*', ie cross-
harrowed. After harrowing came rolling, and in the meantime the *yavel* was
also being broken in, sown and harrowed.

Cast-iron rollers were used in more recent times, and rollers of granite
earlier on. These cylinders of granite had a hole bored at each end and into
these were inserted short metal rods, the *gudges*, to act as axles. They were
held in place by molten lead, poured in from, for example, the lower shell of
an *iley-lamp* or *crusie*, the spout of which was well suited for such a job.

The shafts of a roller were on the couples of the sheaf-end of the barn. The
roller had been of cast-iron, with twin cylinders, made by Banff Foundry. It
was lent to a neighbouring farmer and got broken. The small granite roller at
Brownhill was pulled by a light *shalt*.

Harrows were normally worked in pairs, and were drawn by a pair of
horses. Behind each horse was a 3-ft swingletree, and to these was fixed the
5-ft yoke. A chain about 1½-ft long with a swivel in the middle, ran from the

centre loop of the yoke to the harrow yoke, to each end of which the harrows were attached by an S-hook. The harrows themselves were joined to each other by a pair of loops and shackles in such a way that they could ride up and down differentially over unevennesses. The metal tines of grass-seed harrows did not protrude as far as those of the heavier harrows.

Next came work on the *neep-grun'*. On 3 April, grass-seed was got from Hutcheon in Turriff, along with clover seeds and 4 bushels of rye-grass from Aberdeen. On the next day, 'we turned corn on loft and weighed up to sow neep ground and mixed clover and grass-seed we got 4 bus. ayrshire and mixed through we have 22 bus. for sowing'. A quarter of 'big corn' was got from Uppermill on 8 April, and sown, and 2 quarters more on 24 April. Harrowing and rolling went on as required. Some *bere* as well as corn was sown on the neep ground.

Tares were sown at the end of the *neep* ground, and the grass-seed was sown on the north side and harrowed in with the light, short-tined grass-seed harrow. The sowing machine was ready to be put away on 2 May. The 1929 *Diary*, therefore, shows the sequence of sowing with follow-up activities to have been the lea, the *yavel*, the *neep* ground, and the areas for grass-seed.

Towards the end of April, grubbing, and *straking* with the heavier harrow before the grubber, got into their stride in preparation for the root crops. Some Golden Wonder potatoes were got from Uppermill to plant. May was a month of grubbing, harrowing, rolling, gathering weeds and setting up drills for potatoes first, and then for turnips, both yellows and swedes, the latter job continuing well through June, and there was also *shimmin'* of drills to be done, to clear them of weeds.

By this time the grass fields were well and truly greening, and the first sown grain and turnips were beginning to *breer*. The beasts were let out of the byres, but not all at once. Comments from Mr Hunter's *Diary*, however succinct, show very clearly a farmer's attitude to these essential happenings, especially in adverse weather:

8 April	'grass is looking green and turnip tops coming great speed.'
13 April	'corn offering to brier.'
9 May	'got stirks out at dinner time.'
10 May	'grass is offering to grow some.'
19 May	'things are offering to grow some today, we left 6 stirks outside tonight.'
20 May	'put out 6 two year olds today first time.'
1 June	'everything is terrible dried up just sown turnips has disappeared, terrible dustie roads with motors.'

2 June	'a real wet day took in horse forenoon we was in want of rain ground very dry and faired up in the afternoon and turned out mild kind crops will benefit a lot the ground is got a good sloackin.'
6 June	'corn is started to grow.'
8 June	'corn offering to grow fine now.'
9 June	'turnips offering to brier some.'
13 June	'2 stots still in byre put them on to grass today, cutting grass and corn is offering to raff up now looks like to be a big crop.'
16 June	'turnips very backward.'
17 June	'turnips not doing well we will have to sow some more again.'
19 June	'so we are a kind of finished (with turnips), some of them very doubtful.'
21 June	'crops are looking great dark colour.'

As the time for the stock to go out to graze came nearer, fences had to be seen to where necessary. Fences were generally called *palin's*, and the wire (*weer*) stapled on to the posts was plain or *pykit*.

If new posts were to be put in, an iron *pinch* was used to make the first opening in the ground. The post, set in place, was hammered in with the

25   Jim Hunter using the *peer-man* to tighten a wire.

heavy *mell*. If an old post was to be removed, a 4-ft long *tramp-pick* with a foot-step and a slightly angled point made a useful lever. The one here came from Tollo Croft where Mr Hunter's father lived when working at Carlincraig, and has the name 'Watt' stamped on the side. Watt was a smith at Fortrie at one time.

At gate-openings and field corners there were heavy *strainers* or *strainin' posts*, often sections of old railway sleepers. The wire had to be tightened by hauling it round these, and for this purpose various ingenious devices were developed. The *taings* was a 2-ft long pair of levers hinged at one end, at the point where the wire was gripped. The *orra-man* or *peer-man*, or simply *lever* (pronounced 'laiver') were iron levers of about the same length, with a device near the end for gripping the wire. Though rope pulleys and other patent wire-straining devices eventually replaced these, they were still kept for odd patching jobs. For getting staples out of posts, a 10-in long *picker* served. It was made of an old *risp*, and had a slightly angled and pointed end that slipped into the loop of the staple, or could be hammered into it if the staple had been battered flat against the wire.

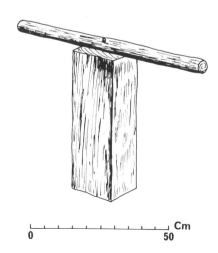

26 A *picker* for extracting staples.   27 A *bishop* for firming loose earth.

When a new *strainer* was put in place, this involved digging a hole into which it was sunk, and the base packed around with stones and earth so that it would stay firm. To consolidate the loosened soil here, or in packing a drain or the like, a heavy wooden *bishop* with a stout handle was used to dump down the earth. The Brownhill one was an upright rectangular block of wood, but a common form was the iron hub of an old cart wheel, into which a wooden handle had been inserted. The process was called *bishopin'*.

EASTER EGGS AN' APRIL EERAN'S

In the middle of this period, youngsters appeared on the scene again at *Pace*. On *Pace Sunday*, they rolled eggs, whose shells were painted, or simply dyed in tea. Sometimes they were dyed yellow with the juice of *funs*, or red with beetroot. The date was established in verse:

> First comes Cannlemass an' syne 'e new meen,
> That meen oot an' 'e neesht meen's hicht,
> The first Sunday efter that's ay Pace richt.

The first of April, *April Feel's* (Fool's) *Day*, was another time when young folk and sometimes gullible adults got a little more attention than usual, through various attempts to send them on *April Eerans*, for example to buy a tin of 'tartan paint', or to borrow a 'bee's halter'. The old chestnut was to say to someone, 'yer pints is lowse', and make them look down. If they did, the cry was 'A ha, ye April Feel!'

28   Brownhill, Easter 1983.

33

THE HEY

'The hey' was the first of the harvests, dealt with in July, and on into August if the weather was poor. The 1938 *hey hairst* was almost completely within July, that for 1923 was mainly in August:

31 July	'started to turn hay afternoon and put up some small coles not in order, gathered a bitie and stooked it up for seed.'
2 Aug	'Willie raking and I turned some rakins we put up a few coles and cut some seed.'
4 Aug	'we wrought or nearly 10 o'clock at night I got it cut and stooked up.'
15 Aug	'Jim raked the founds of coles with Mr Hutcheon's rake and took home load of rakins finished. Willie and me put thatch round top of hay coles that was thrashed.'
20 Aug	'Drew the haystacks and got two thacked.'

29   Mowing hay with a horse-mower adapted for the tractor. A *side-rake* is being used, 1962.

34

30   Work in the hay-field, 1962.

31   Twisting a *thoom-raip* for a cole, 1962.

Once cut, the hay was left to lie for a time in order to dry in the swathe, sometimes being turned with forks. With care, the handle could be slipped under the swathe so that sections could be turned at once. It was a time when an anxious eye was kept on rain clouds.

When judged dry enough the swathes were gathered into long *winraas* by means of a rake or *tummlin-tam*, and the rows were then gathered sideways into clumps by the same implements, to assist the folk who were *coling*.

If there was a risk of wind, a *thoom-raip* was twisted by hand out of the side of the *cole*, taken over the top, and tied in at the far side. The *coles* could be carted home after this, to be built into *hey-rucks*, or a number of small *coles* could be combined, still in the field, into larger *tramp-coles*, though this was not a practice at Brownhill.

When the *coles* had been *led*, the rake was again used to get all the loose hay, the *rakins*, gathered up, and these were also kept. In place of a horse-rake, a shoulder-rake, the *smiler*, might be used. It was heavy to pull and had a strap or sack-covered rope going round the shoulder to give extra traction power. 'Fit wye wid it be ca'd a smiler?' 'Weel, ye widna be smilin' if ye'd tae pull't lang.'

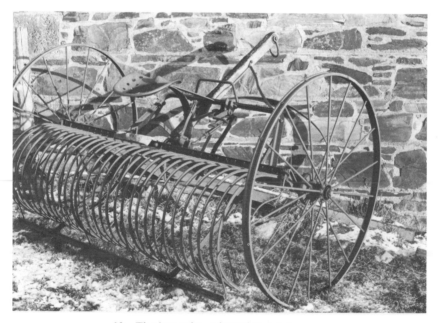

32   The hay-rake, adapted to tractor use.

For dragging *coles* to the stacking site, the horse-drawn *tummlin-tam* was also used. It was made by Alex Jack & Sons Ltd, Maybole, in Ayrshire, and had been bought at an Agricultural Show in Aberdeen. It fell out of use after hay began to be baled, but in its *potestatur*, the horse could drag complete *hey-coles* to the cornyard with it. Once there, the men driving it raised the two handles, the wooden forks caught in the ground, and the whole contraption tumbled over the top of the cole and back onto an even keel at the other side, leaving the hay behind.

Surplus hay, or hay taken from the stacks for use as winter fodder, was carted into the close and filled into the *hey-laft*, the door to which was above the *neep-shed* door in a dormer window-like extension to the roof. In the apex of this extension was a *doocot*. Another door in the hay-loft opened into the stable at the level of the couples.

Some hay in earlier days was scythed and stooked to be threshed out for grass-seed.

33   On the right is the hay-loft, above the *neep*-shed. On the left is the *chaamer*, then the gig-shed with sliding doors, then the stable door. Easter 1983.

THE NEEPS

Neeps was a general term that covered both *yallas* and *swads* or Swedish turnips. *Neep shaavin'* took place in May and early June, using a horse-drawn, two-drill *neep shaaver*. This had two light cast-iron rollers and a full-width wooden roller behind, from the centre of which the two seed boxes were turned by a chain round a wooden pulley. It was pulled by a single horse, and the driver walked behind it, between a pair of light handles. It was constructed by Mennie, blacksmith at Fortrie Smiddy, after Mr Hunter came to Brownhill. The two *spoots* of the machine ran on top of the *dreels* that the *dreel-ploo* had made, the flow of seed from the rotating seed boxes being adjusted to the state of the soil. Drills always ran up and down the slope, for drainage.

When the *neep-seed* germinated and the young shoots appeared, they were sometimes attacked by the turnip fly, or else excessive drought stopped them in their tracks, leaving bare stretches in the drill. In that case a hand-tool called a *Bobbin John* or *patcher* was used to re-sow. This could take two forms. One was commercial, consisting of a rotating perforated drum on the end of a long handle. The other was home-made from an old cocoa tin with a perforated base, tied to the end of a stick, filled with seed and shaken along the drill. That this kind of device was over a century old in the area is shown by an entry for 7 July 1853 in the *Diary* of a farmer from Chapelpark,

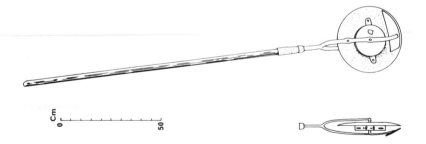

34   A *Bobbin' John* for sowing turnip seed.

Methlick: 'Sowed some neeps with hand box.' In fact, it is much older, for it appears to have been introduced by Mr Udny of Udny around 1730. According to a description dated 1794, turnip seed was shaken onto the drills from a box of plated tin, 9 in long by 1 in diameter (22.8 × 2.5 cm), with a slip cover at one end held by a catch. There were three or four holes in the end, each big enough for a seed. The box was flat at one end so as to be fixed to a handle, a rod with a knobbed end, to prevent slipping. In use it was half-filled, and gently shaken along the drills.

From mid-June till mid-July, the painstaking task of *hyowin'*, sometimes called *singlin'*, went on, drill by drill so that the plants could be spaced to permit growth and as far as possible be selected for strength. A number of men worked together in echelon, each with his long-handled *hyow*. Hoed out plants and weeds like *knot girse* were thrust into the hollows between the drills, where the growth of weeds had been destroyed by the *shim* during the sowing period, and the crop was then left to grow and swell until the time came to use it for the cattle after they were stalled for the winter in the *byre*, ie 'aifter 'e beas' wis teen in'. This happened as a rule in the third quarter of October, or later if the weather was good, and in preparation Mr Hunter

35 Hoeing turnips, 1966.

recorded on 26 June 1929: 'over at Mennie's smiddy got scythe blades put on hoes.' Old scythes, therefore, were made use of as hoe blades.

Turnip work then rested till Autumn. *Diary* entries for two days in November (and one for January), 'furrin up neeps', shows that the drill plough was being used to get earth around the roots as a protection from frost, but the main effort from October till late April or May went into regular pulling and carting of turnips into the *neep-shed* at the end of the byre. In March and April came the final 'liftin'', to leave the fields clear for preparation for the crops to follow.

Pu'in neeps was a task that needed much persistence. It was done by hand with the aid of two tools, one held in each hand, a *neep-click* and a *tapner* or *tailer*. The *click* was sometimes entirely of metal, even for the hand grip, and had a two-pronged hook at the end which was swung into the body of the turnip to hoist it from the drill. In soft weather the turnips were pulled by hand by grasping the *shaas*, but the *click* came into play during times of

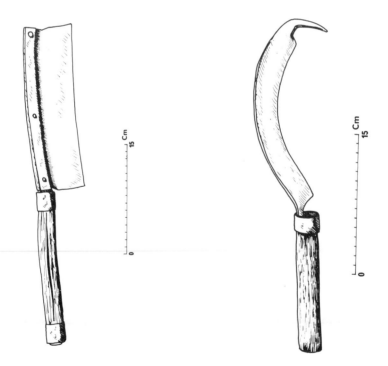

36 A *tapner* or *tailer* made from a scythe-blade.

37 A commercially-supplied *tapner* or *tailer*.

frost. This is also evidenced in another *Diary* from a neighbouring part of Buchan. On 4 January 1869, George Gall of Oldtown, Atherb, was 'pulling and driving turnips we was obliged to pull them with Cleeks as the old frost prevented them from pulling with our hands'.

The terms *tapner* and *tailer* were used interchangeably, one referring to cutting of the tops and the other the tails or roots of the turnips. The tool had a wooden handgrip, and those commercially supplied usually had a single hook at the end of a stout blade. If the strengthening strip of metal along the back of a segment of scythe blade came loose through wear, Mr Hunter would take it to the blacksmith (nicknamed 'Brooky') to get it *clinkit*. The smith also made new ones, as on 12 April 1929: 'at Fortrie Smidy 3 socks and coulter laid and 3 tailers made.'

Brooky made the all-iron *neep-clicks*, but those with wooden handles were either home-made or bought from the blacksmith or ironmonger. Another essential tool was the *neep-pluck*, which had a stout wooden handle about 3 ft long, and a heavy, two-pronged or mattock-shaped head of iron, with which turnips could be plucked or levered from the drills in deep snow or in particularly hard frost. In some cases, when sheep had been put on to eat off the turnips in a field, the *pluck* was used by the shepherd to get the remaining roots up for his flock to eat. Mr Hunter used an old leather *mitten* when working the *pluck*. Land which had been cleared of turnips and was being used for a following grain crop was called the *neep-reet* and the crop was *neep-corn*.

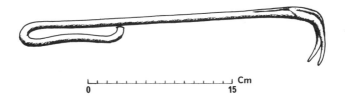

38   A smith-made *neep-click*, all iron.

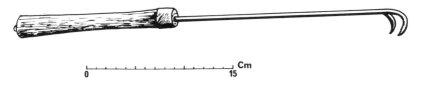

39   A wooden-handled *neep-click*.

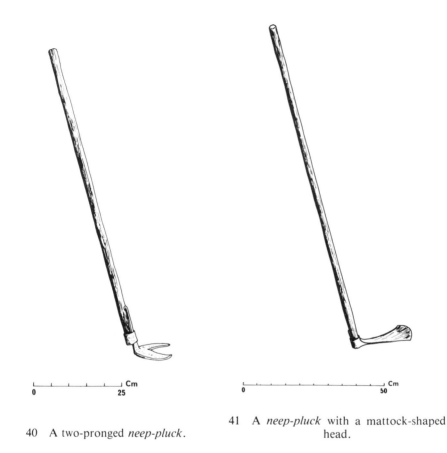

| | Cm |
| 0 | 25 |

| | Cm |
| 0 | 50 |

40   A two-pronged *neep-pluck*.

41   A *neep-pluck* with a mattock-shaped head.

Turnips were lifted in such a way that there was space for the horse and cart to come betweeen the rows of pulled turnips, which were then thrown into the cart from two sides. Back at the steading, the cart was backed into the *neep-shed*, the *back door* was taken off, and the load was *coupit* on to the *cassied* floor.

The *neep-shed* had double sliding doors to allow access by carts from the *close*, and another door, counterbalanced to slide vertically up and down, that led through to the cow-byre. Two piles of turnips, yellows and swedes,were made. Alongside stood the iron-shod wheel-barrow, and the iron *neep-hasher*. The *hasher* was on four legs, high enough for the barrow to be pushed underneath to receive the slices that fell through a grating of sharp blades as the plunger was brought down on each turnip. The operator

42   A row of neeps, with *tapner* and *pluck*.

held a *neep-click* in one hand and *clickit up* neeps from the pile, one at a time, to feed the *hasher*. The slices were gathered in a wooden or openwork wire *backet* that was set in the barrow, and were then carried to the byre for the calves that had just been *coggit*. This backet was probably the one bought at Anderson the smith's *roup*, when he went out of Pitglassie Smiddy, to be followed by Gideon Irvine.

43   An iron *neep-hasher*.

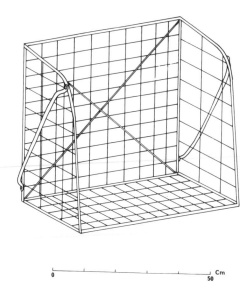

44   A wire *backet*.

Cm

0   40

45   A wooden *backet*.

For the most part, the cattle got whole turnips, but sliced turnips were required for any that had difficulty, for some reason, in *howking neeps* for themselves. Apart from the big, iron *hashers*, there were also smaller, home-made *han' hashers*, consisting of a wooden frame to the top of which a blade (often an old scythe blade) was hinged at one end, to act as a slicer.

THE HAIRST

August was the slackest month, when odd jobs could be done, doors and windows could be painted in red or blue, and *sprots* cut in the bog for later use in thatching stacks. If the weather had been good, the *hairst* could start, the first step being the 'reddin' o' roads' round the sides of the field , using the scythe, so that the binder could enter without running over the standing corn.

Reaping with a *hyeuk* was long over by Mr. Hunter's time, but the scythe remained in active use. This was the type with a Y-shaped *sned* with two handgrips, and a blade fixed to the end of the shaft by means of an iron ferrule and wedge, and a single metal strut, the *grass-hyeuk* or *girse-hyeuk*. In latter days the blade was sharpened with a long carborundum *scythe-steen*, round in section, but earlier on with a bat-shaped, wooden *scythe-brod* or *straik*, with an emery mixture attached to each side. The scythes were supplied by the local blacksmith.

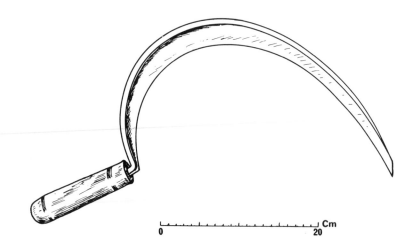

46   A reaping hook.

46

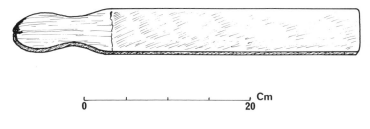

0   20 Cm

47   A *scythe-brod*.

Mr Hunter related that during scything, 'fin corn wis stannin' gey stracht up, it wis like tae fa' i' the bout an' mak a lot o' rakins, especially gin 'ere wis nae win'. A loon wis got tae walk alangside 'e scythesman wi' a gad—a rodden stick or a bittie o' saach wid be fine—an' held it awa' fae 'e blade so 'at 'e corn wid fa' richt.' He had heard of this, but had not seen it done. By the time he left school, binders had come in and the scything of entire crops was finished, though the scythe continued for *reddin roads* around fields. 'Cuttin' roads' is mentioned in his 1937 *Diary* on 31 August and 1 September only. This was an average to good year, but not so 1938, when stormy weather *laid* much of the crop. Then the scything of roads and flattened patches went on, alongside cutting with the binder. The entry for 22 August is 'start hairst, corn flat'. Scything is mentioned on 24 to 31 August inclusive (31 August: 'scythin roads on clean land') and 1, 2 and 8 September, ie 11 days in all, and the lea was actually cut with the mower in this year, on 6, 10, 12, 14 and 15 September, before they 'took *Clyack*' on 19 September.

In the days before the binder, three or four scythes would normally work together on a three-pair *toon*. The horsemen handled them. If three scythes were in use, there would be three women gathering. They gathered, made the band, and laid the sheaf on it, but did not tie the band. This was the job for the two men who 'bun' an' stookit', serving the three *bouts*. Each man, therefore, served a *bout* and a half. They took the centre *bout* sheaf about, 'ilky secont shafe i' the middle bout', and called that a 'scythe an' a half'. The women were *lifters* or *gaitherers*, and the men were *ban'sters*.

In the days of the scythe, if the corn was badly laid and twisted, it was not possible for the scythers to work neatly one behind the other. 'They vrocht rig an' rig—they hid gey nerra rigs at 'at time. There wis fyles a gey hash tae see fa'd gotten throwe 'eir rig first.'

After the horse-drawn reaper came into use, *lifters* and *ban'sters* worked behind it also, but 'it wis a gey hing-in ahin a reaper'. Binders came in after the reaper, self-knotting so that the need to tie bands virtually disappeared. With the binder, five *bouts* was the common thing for *stooking*.

The topic led to a reminiscence about Francis Finnie, grieve and manager at the farm of Tollo. He was a character, who wore moleskin breeks that were always 'as fite's a doo (dove) on Monday mornin''. When they first got a binder he said: 'I dinna ken foo we'll get on this hairst, we've got een o' yon binner things.' In the words of Mr Hunter, 'He wis a queer kinna lad, fyles it (the crop) widna been in verra great order, he wid 'a been leadin, idder days fin ither fowk wis leadin', he widna been leadin. He nivver wore a flannen just a cotton sark. He wore a shaftit weskit (also called the *shafter*). He nivver hid bit ae pair o' mittens an' 'e sellt them at a profit, ye'd see 'im on 'e caalest day teerin up at 'e neeps wi' 'is bare han's. If 'e wis wirkin' doon on 'e laich grun near a burn on a warm simmer day an' 'e wis thirsty, he widna teen a drink. "Oh'', he says, "I micht be awa up on 'e hill 'e neist day far I couldna get a drink.'' Fyles if ye met in wi' 'im he'd 'a' newsed, neist time he'd nivver 'a' spoken. Great big strong chiel. I div a kinna min' on 'im, he'd 'a' been in ma father's time.'

The reaping machine on the farm in the 1950s, was one made by Harrison, McGregor & Co Ltd, of Leigh, Lancashire. The binder was a Bisset, bought at Michie's roup at Uppermill in 1922. However cut, the crop of oats or *bere* was set up into *stooks*. Each *stook* consisted of five pairs of sheaves, though sometimes on the *clean lan'* only four pairs were set up, because of the grassy sole. It was easier to shift eight sheaves to a new stance, two men taking four sheaves a-piece, so that the grass should not be spoiled by having *stooks* staying too long in one place. In this area the injunction was 'stook aye tae Bennachie', because *stooks* aligned with that hill lay north and south for maximum exposure, and would *win* better.

There was a story about Willie Tocher o' Yokieshill. He 'couldna see Bennachie, sae he just stookit tae Mormon' Hill. The fairmer he gee'd roon. "Aye Tocher'', he says, "that's nae 'e wye tae stook.'' "Weel, I couldna see Bennachie, sae I just stookit tae Mormon'.'''

The tail of the sheaf was the *butt*. The word *gavel* was also known, but only through its currency in the song, *Johnny Sangster*. The proper way to *stook* the sheaves was to set them with the knot of the band to the inside, so that the *shear* of the butt lay to the outside and the smallest possible area sat on the ground. With a straw band, it was the corn ends that were 'knottit', and the corny knots were set in to prevent them from growing 'in a *weety* time'. With binder sheaves, Mr Hunter normally *stooked* with the knot out. As he said, they sat better like this, but all the same there was a better run on the sheaf with the knot in and this was probably the best way to do it. About three weeks was the average time for drying in the stook.

One of the least pleasant jobs during harvest was *stook parade*, when *stooks* demolished by storm and wind had to be set up again. The *stookers* inevitably got a thorough soaking. Mr Hunter noted such occasions in his *Diary*. The stooks were levelled on 12 September 1937, for example, and had to be set up again on the two days after. On the 19th, he noted: 'Stockie [sic] Sunday in New Deer district.' The discomfort of the job is clear.

In pre-tractor days, leading with horse and cart took a considerable time. The farm had three horses and two carts then. Two horses and two carts required four folk to work to them: 'a forker on 'e lan', a bigger on ilky cairt, an' een biggin 'e rucks'. The Brownhill practice was for Mr Hunter to do the skilled job of building the stacks, the *fee't man* took one cart, one *quarterer* the other, and another man did the forking.

There was a small cart and a large cart at the farm. the small one, with frame and shelvings, came from Carlincraig, and the larger was bought at a roup at Quarryhill, Monquhitter. Carts were of basic importance in farm work, and were well looked after. About July, when the driving of dung was over, they were given a good wash.

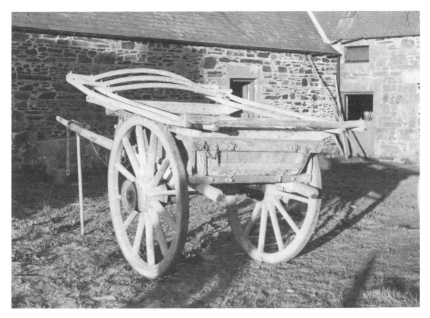

48   Cart with harvest-frame and resting-pole, 1960.

They were open box-carts, adapted by various fitments to a wide range of purposes and achieving a high degree of versatility. The front and sides of the body were fixed, and the tail-board or *back-door* was movable so that loads could be *cowpit* when the body was raised. The front board was the 'breist o' 'e cairt'.

For loads like turnips, *shelvin's* were added to the sides to give greater depth: two *side-shelvin's*, a *front-shelvin'*, and a *hin'-shelvin'*. For hay, straw and sheaves a rectangular wooden *frame* was laid over the body, of such a kind that loads could be built out all round beyond the body.

Underneath the body, providing the main supports, were two *lyin'-shafts*; they sat on top of the *aixle*, which was held in position by two long *garron-nails* that ran through the 'fleer o' 'e cairt'. They were each held in place by a pin and ring that went through the slots in their lower ends, beneath the axle. When these pins were removed, the cart could be lifted off its axle. The horse was harnessed between the shafts, and beneath one of them was fastened the *restin' pole*. It could be swung down so that the end touched the ground, when it acted as a prop to support the weight of the cart and give the horse a rest for a while. This was especially needed on long, heavy draughts for peat, coal and the like.

The iron attachments on the shaft included the *sliders* with hooks into which the *back-cheyn*, passing over the *saiddle*, fitted. There were also the *fore-slings*, on the front of the iron bars on the shafts, for attaching the hooks on the harness. The *hin'-slings* at the rear, however, were not fixed to the shafts but to the *britchin'*, and were linked to the hooks at the back ends of the iron rods on the shafts.

The links on the *fore-slings* were of different sizes, smaller nearer the shaft and bigger away from it, and there was also a swivel in the chain. The difference in size of the links was to make it easier to fit the *slings* into the *hyeuk* of the *haim* on the collar. 'There wid be fower or five big links an' ye wid say, "Foo many links are ye hingin'?"' If you said three, then three links were left free beyond the hook. 'Ye hid tae study that, nae tae hae 'e horse ower far forrit if they were ower slack, an' if they were ower ticht 'e cairt wid be kinna pushin' 'e horse.'

The wheels themselves consisted of the nave, the spokes, the *fillies*, and the iron rings.

The 1937 *Diary* shows that in that year, harvesting with the binder started on 27 August, roads having been *redd* with the scythe around the fields, the *yavel* being cut first and then the *clean lan'*. As it happened, no *ley* had been *crappit* in that year. Cutting finished on 7 August, and leading followed with its usual urgency. All was in by 22 September.

49   Granite stack-foundation.

When forking onto the cart, a skilful forker could help the *bigger* by turning the sheaves with his fork so that they not only lay to hand, but also in the right position for being built into *gyangs* above the frame of the cart, or for *hertin*, ie filling in the heart. In the field the two-pronged fork was full-sized, of the type used for either straw or hay, but for forking at the *ruck*, where the correct positioning of sheaves was more critical, and only one at a time was forked, a *shafe-fork* was often used. Its prongs were around 2½ in apart and just under 5 in long. The small size let the sheaf slip off easily. It was also more useful than the standard forks for shoving in the tails of sheaves when tidying a *ruck* that was being built.

When corn was being cut or led, the *piece* was taken to the fields by one of the women of the house. A special treat then was *honey ale*, made quite often at Brownhill and kept in the milkhouse. Comb honey was put in a muslin bag and allowed to drip. The comb left in the bag was steeped. Then a slice of bread was toasted, yeast was put on top, and this was floated on the liquid strained off after steeping and put in a pot. The pot was left to sit for three days to a week. After that the liquid was bottled and left for a day or two when it was ready for drinking, but it was often very volatile and apt to blow the corks. Half the bottle was often lost in the field because it frothed so rapidly.

When all the corn had been led and the fields were left with clean *stibble*, a neighbour might say, 'Ay, ye've gotten winter.'

Similarly for the end of cutting, the phrase was 'ye've gotten clyack', but Mr Hunter had experienced no special ceremonies with regard to the *clyack shafe*.

In the *cornyard*, the rucks were built on *foons*, usually consisting of a circle of stones covered with branches or broom, or simply a layer of branches arranged in a circle. More rarely there were foundations made of a circle of stone uprights of Peterhead granite, and one in the centre, each with a granite cap so that they looked like stone mushrooms. Spars of wood were laid across. On these, stacks could be built completely clear of the ground.

A single fencing post was hammered into the centre of the *foon* with the *mell* (heavy-headed hammer), if such stones were not being used.

When building began, sheaves were *stooked* against this post, if there was one (it was not needed for a good, dry crop), so that the *hert* could be kept well up. Sheaves were added all round, at a continually lessening angle, until the outer ring was reached. This made the first *gyang*. The basic principle to be observed as the *ruck* grew was always to keep the heart up so that water would run off along the lie of the stalks. In Angus and Southeast Scotland, there were much bigger stacks with wide bodies that rose for some distance before the head began to be formed but, in the North East generally, the inwards curve began more or less at shoulder level. At this point, the builder started *draain' in*, making the *gyangs* a little smaller in circumference each time he went round, until at last there was room for only the *heedin shafe*. This was often stood on its head, and the tail curled down over the band.

The point at which *draain' in* began was at the *easin's*. Some specialists who took pride in their work sometimes built the *easin gyang* farther out than the others, so that it slightly overhung the *gyangs* below it. In this case it was known as the *turned gyang*, with the shear of the sheaf underneath. A main practical reason was that it helped with *thackin* or *theekin*. The *thack* was carried down to this point and slightly beyond, so that it threw water well clear.

In a busy cornyard a man was given the job of keeping an eye on the shape of the stacks, pulling out a sheaf here, pushing in another there with a fork, and making sure that all was on the plumb. If, in spite of all, the stack tilted a little to one side, one or more *ruck-posts* had to be leaned against it as supports. 'That ruck wid need an oxter-stav' was a jocular reference to a leaning stack, implying derision of the builder.

50   Thatching a stack with rushes from the bog, 1959.

There was a wooden rake with a 6-ft long shaft and a 2-ft wide head with thirteen 3-in tines, mainly used for tidying up the cornyard. It was bought at Gideon Irvine's roup, when he left Pitglassie Smiddy and went over to Fortrie, and was thought to have been made by him.

The thatch was of *sprots* or *rashes*, cut in the bog alongside the burn below the farm shortly before they were required. They were laid green. *Strae* from the year before might also be used. It was laid in place from a *ruck-ledder*, and the next and final stage was to *raip* it down well against the winter storms.

At one time, a double-thick *raip*, the *bag-raip*, was fixed around the stack at, or just below, the *easin*. Another name for this was the *eave raip*. The *raips* on the *heid o' 'e ruck* were taken once round the *bag-raip* before being

51   Twisting a straw-rope with a *thraa hyeuk*, 1959.

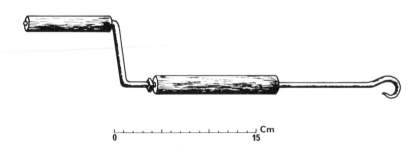

52   A *thraa hyeuk*.

tied into the side of the stack. Latterly *bag-raips* were not used and the ends of the *raips* were simply tied in, the end of the *raip* and a tuft of straw from the tail of a stacked sheaf being twisted together till the *raip* was tight, and the end tucked in behind it.

Raipin' 'e thack was a sophisticated exercise. First of all, the *raips* were twisted in the barn during wet days, of straw or latterly of binder-twine, by means of a metal twister shaped like a car-starting handle, with two wooden handgrips within which the body rotated. This was the *thraa-hyeuk*, *thraa-crook*, or *twiner*. An older form of twister was a rod with a walking-stick shaped head that acted as a hook, and at the other end a swivel that provided a hand hold. It was generally called a *tweezler* or *tweezlick*, and was made of 'hard wun saach'. A piece of *tow* across the head served as a stay to hold the curve firm so that the straw did not slip off, and also to keep the *raip* from slipping into the middle of the hook. Use of the *tweezlick* required a good deal of motion with the hand that held it along its 2-ft length. If the operator was used to it, a good job could be done, and not everyone liked the smoother-turning, innovative crank-shaped twisters at first. As Mr Hunter said, 'some fowk took ill wi' this thraa-crooks fin they cam in first'.

The job of twisting required least skill. The operator simply moved backwards slowly, twisting as he went. On the straw before him sat the *latter-oot*, the man who fed the straw in an even stream through the space between the thumb and forefinger of one hand, meanwhile using the other fingers to tuck in loose ends and smooth rough patches. It was possible to twist a short rope, a *thoom raip* of hay or straw, for some temporary job, using the hands only. The thumb served as a hook. For this reason there is a saying, 'makin' a thoom raip wi' yer first finger', to indicate an impossibility.

The completed ropes were coiled into round balls called *cloos*, up to the size of a football, or bigger, or else they were twisted with considerable ingenuity into a smaller shuttle-shaped form, about a foot long and containing 12 to 15 ft of rope, called an *edderin*. *Cloos* and *edderins* reflected two forms of thatching, the first called *swappin* and the second *edderin*. In *swappin*, *raips* were laid alternately across the shoulders of the stack, using the *cloos*, so that the end result gave a diamond-shaped appearance. In *edderin*, however, ropes were first put on vertically, often three in number to give six uprights, from one side over the top and down to the other, and fixed firmly. Then the specially-shaped *edderin* was used to thread another rope round each of these verticals, from top to bottom, so that the final appearance was one of a set of squares. *Edderin* made a tighter job than *swappin*, but more work was involved and in latter days it became less common.

In applying the *raips*, one man worked off a ladder at the top of the stack and another stood on the ground, ready to catch the *cloo* as it was moved from one side of the stack to the other. Mr Hunter's habit, as he threw the *cloo* down on the opposite side from which it was first thrown up, was to shout 'Look up!' If you did you got it in the face.

53   James Hunter with a newly-made *edderin*, 1959.

A *hairst-supper* was often held when ''e biggin' o' 'e rucks' was finished, before the extra hands had left. It consisted of a meal, something to drink, and maybe some dancing afterwards.

In latter days stacks were not built with the same care and pride, partly because hands were becoming more expensive, and therefore fewer. As *straeraips* were replaced by twisted binder-twine, then by coir-yarn, and finally by nets, the older skills faded, and even stacks are scarcely part of the farming scene any more.

As the year wore on, and the cattle began to be kept again in the byre overnight, the need for straw as food and bedding meant that the summer's respite from threshing was over. In 1937, there was a threshing with the barn mill on 29 September. On 20 October a stack was taken into the barn, and thereafter the driving in of stacks, and their threshing, occupied ten of the November and December days. At the beginning of the same year, between 7 January and 12 August, at least 26 days were taken up with these activities. Even though the taking in of a *ruck* and a threshing occupied up to only half a day in each case, the input of labour was still considerable.

The bulk of the stacks was threshed with the barn mill, but the travelling mill came once a year to clear stacks still left in the cornyard and produce marketable grain. On 7 August 1941, for example: 'Wilson's mill threshing, 28 qrs. Baler working 8 tons straw.' The use of the baler, which shaped the straw into firm rectangular blocks, made a great difference to the ease of handling the straw. Before the baler days, what could not be stored indoors had to be built up into *strae soos* with much effort. Such sows, like hay stacks, compacted after a while and it was not easy to get the hay or straw hauled out with a fork or *graip*. For this reason, a sharp *hey-knife* with a broad or zig-zag blade, or a sharpened spade, were used to slice into the mass to make the cut off parts easier to remove.

Helping neighbours when the travelling mill came was a regular task. As a rule it was the *fee't man* who was sent to help. In 1929, he was at the steam-mill at Curriedown, Midtown of Pitglassie and Pitglassie, ie the adjacent farms, and folk from there would come to help at Brownhill's thresh when that time came. On two occasions in August it was grass-seed that was being threshed at Midtown (pronounced 'Minten') and at Pitglassie ('Pitties').

In normal years the travelling mill came to Brownhill in the summer, often about June. Wilson of Turriff was one of the contractors, and sometimes Easton of Pitcaple or Christie of Rothie Vale (between Rothienorman and Fyvie) were used.

In earlier days there was a steam mill, operated by Duguid ('dyukit') of Arnhead. 'He wis here ae nicht, it cam on an aafa thun'erstorm. They had a

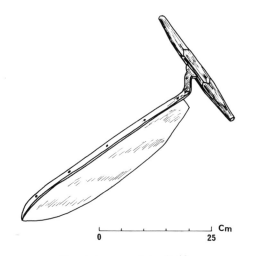

54   A hay- or straw-knife.

larry an' jist beddit up for 'e nicht. Ay there cam on anither flash an' this
lichtit up a dose o' chuckens reestit in 'e boortree. Dyukit couldna
unnerstan' fit 'is wis an' hid tae rise tae gang an' see.'

   At one time two brothers, John and Jimmy Shirran, lived in what was later
the roadman's cottage and finally the *souter's* shop next Pitglassie Smiddy.
John took in orders, and Jimmy was the traction engine man. He drove an
engine called the 'Cock of the North', and there was another called 'Elma'
driven by a man Duffus that they hired. They did not keep their mills and
machinery at the Smiddy, but at some of the Thorneybanks, where they had
been for a while, and before that at Uppermill. There was a very wide
entrance off the road leading to Uppermill, said to allow the mill and engine
to turn in more easily. Willie Beddie, who was farm-servant at Brownhill,
married a daughter of Jimmy Shirran.

   Another traction engine owner was Mr Smart in the Kirktoon o'
Auchterless, across from the Free Kirk Manse. Jimmy Shirran drove for him
later on. Stories about Smart abound. 'He wis an aafa ill-gruntit kinna chiel,
they wid 'a' geen awa till a place, the secint man wirkin' 'e wheel, an' he wid
niver say faar they were gaan. He wid jist say fin they cam till a turnin,
"Turn here!"'

   'Willie Beddie min's on 'im at a mull at Thornybank, they'd gotten soup
till their denner an' fin Smairt wis sittin' doon, 'e plate wis maybe ower near

han' 'e edge o' 'e table, 'an 'e edge o' eez waiskit took it, an' up in eez face.'
''E took some aafa bursts o' drink an' syne 'e secint man had tae cairry on,
'an 'e fairmer hid tae supply an extra man. He kept eez mull an' ingine in
gweed order, though.'

The steam mill towed both the threshing mill and a wooden-sided, four-
wheeled lorry or van, ''e mullman's van', for the men to sleep in. There were
usually two men with it, who took turn about in the careful operation of
feeding the loosened sheaves into the mill. Rough feeding could affect the
quality of the thresh. A common make of travelling mill was the Marshall.
Garvie of Aberdeen was also popular, and was the type used by Easton.

Before the mill came, the farmer had to lay in sacks of coal to keep the
engine fired and the carrying of pails of water as it worked was an 'eident'
job. In the cornyard, hollows had sometimes to be dug to get the mill
completely level: a spirit level attached to the mill was the guide.

About a dozen people were needed to operate the mill: a feeder and two
lowsers (to cut the bands of the sheaves: usually women or young lads) on
top, two forkers or sometimes three, three men for handling the corn (or two
if only *setting by* was being done), and others for handling the straw.

55   The travelling-mill, 1966.

Neighbouring was regularly done with Uppermill and Mid Pitglassie, and Ackie Gray from a Hill of Hatton croft always came, as well as his father Sandy (who acted as local molecatcher) as long as he was able.

Before the days of *bunchers* attached to the end of the mill to tie the straw into bunches for easier handling, the straw was carried loose up a long elevator to the *strae-soo*. Bunches were also hoisted on the elevator for stacking. More recently the baler became a standard part of the rig and, because of the greater compression, much more straw could be stored in barns and byres than before, and fewer regular threshings with the barn mill were needed.

Food was provided on the day the mill came. The greatly awaited moment in the morning or afternoon was the arrival of the *piece*, when the women came with baskets of baps and scones spread with butter and jam, and tea kettles full of tea, with plenty of milk and sugar. No one drank tea without these. Good dinners were provided at midday, though stories were rife about thrifty farmers' wives who tried to make things go as far as possible. *Stame-mull breid* was a well-kown product, oatcakes, baked thick with too much bicarbonate of soda, and greenish in the middle, to discourage the men from eating too much. 'Twa breids an' a brose' was a local name for this delicacy.

At one mill dinner, 'they aa sat doon tae some broth an' 'e wife said, "It wis jist a dwinin' hennie bit it made fine maamie broth." They said 'e men aa geed oot.'

The travelling mill started to come round in Mr Hunter's father's time, in the third quarter of the nineteenth century. As he put it, 'At 'e start o' 'e traivellin' mull, they hid tae haal them wi' 'e horse. They didna ken much foo tae dee wi' 'em an' they'd gotten an Englishman tae gie them a han'. At ae place 'e got milk-broth an' 'e says, "We got milk-broth tae wir denner bit I just gave them a milk-broth thresh." He wis aafa ill aboot whisky, if ye'd jist noticet 'im wi' a suppie whisky at 'e time, ye'd gotten a gran' thrash. They were aakwird kinna things tae work wi' the horse. He geed till 'e back door at Cyarlins eence an' asked for a drink. They offered 'im ale, bit 'e said, "It's rather soft." It wis whisky he wis wintin'.' The same Englishman heard once of another threshing outfit that had newly started up, with a thresher that he regarded as small and ineffective. 'Oh', he said, 'the wee weelies (wheels) of her, ye widna waddlet it in three days.' Interestingly, the English de-aspiration of *wh-* is remembered in this century-old story, even though much of the saying has been scotticised otherwise.

For weighing up the corn at the travelling-mill, the weighing-machine was always brought down from the loft, complete with its *wechts*, including the 'fifty-sixers' used by farm folk to demonstrate their strength by swinging them straight-armed above their heads, preferably one in each hand.

56   *Piece-time* at the *mull*, 1966

57   At the threshing mill, 1966.

Though some *bere* was grown, the bulk of the crop was *tattie-corn*, grown in three shifts totalling about 33 acres. Latterly much of this was sold to Scottish Agricultural Industries at Station Road, Turriff, but when a fresh stock of oatmeal was needed for porridge, *brose* and oatcakes, about 4 qr were sent over to the Mill of Newmill in Auchterless for grinding. 'They eest tae spik aboot hale meal, ye got aboot a bow (boll) an' a half tae the quarter. It didna aye mull 'e same. Syne 'ere wis 'e dist an' sids.' The *dist* and *sids* were used for feeding livestock, and the dish called *sowens* was made from *sids*, after they had been put through a special *sowen's sieve* to get rid of the pieces of husk.

When the oat meal came home it was put into the *girnel* in the *chaamer* and packed in as firmly with the fists as possible to help to make it keep. This girnel was bought at the roup of Duguid of Arnhead. Where there was a big *girnel*, it was tramped with the feet, and Mr Hunter remembered tramping in the meal with his bare feet at Carlincraig. His father would say: 'Meal wis the only thing that ye took oot mair than ye pit in.'

58   Mill of Newmill, Auchterless.

THE BYRE

With the end of harvest, hopefully in October if the weather allowed, the round of ploughing and indoor byre work began again. With straw, turnips and hay in store, the winter fodder was assured.

In the byre, the *staa's*, most of them for holding two animals, were separated by wooden *trevises*. In the front of each stall, there was a *troch* at floor level. It was into this that turnips were tipped from the *backet*, or if the turnips still had fresh shaws on them, they could be thrown by hand up between the beasts into the *troch*. This was the job of the *bylie* or cattleman. Above the *troch*, angled against the wall at the head height of the animals, was an open-work slatted wooden frame, the *heck*, into which went the other major components of the animals' diet, straw from the barn, or hay. The whole front area, including *troch* and *heck*, was the *forestaa*.

59 Mucking the beasts.

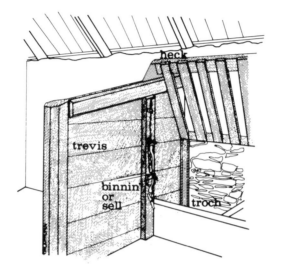

60   Details of the stall.

Incorporated in the *trevis*, in line with the front of the *troch*, was a strong wooden upright into which the iron *slider* that held the cattle fastenings was bolted. The *sliders* averaged 16 in long, which allowed the animal to raise and lower its head to whatever extent it wanted. These items were made and repaired in the smiddy: 'I was over at Mennies smidy afternoon and got 5 new sliders and a few repaired and bindings repaired' (15 August 1929).

The fastening itself was the *binnin'* or *sell*. This consisted of a length of chain, attached to the *slider* by a stout loop, and about 20 inches long, called the *thrammle* or *trammle*. At its other end was a *sweevle* with a big loop into which the chain round the animal's neck was fixed. This neck chain was opened and closed by means of an iron pin and loop. This was the most common form of *sell*, but there was also a variety used for animals that became too clever and learned how to draw their heads out of the chain. This was a band of solid iron, the *bowsell* that went round the neck and was very firmly fastened below with an iron catch.

The floor of the stall had no special name in this area other than the *staa*. The slightly hollowed drain or gutter at the back of the animals was the *greep*, along which the *strang* flowed out to the *strang-hole* in the *midden*.

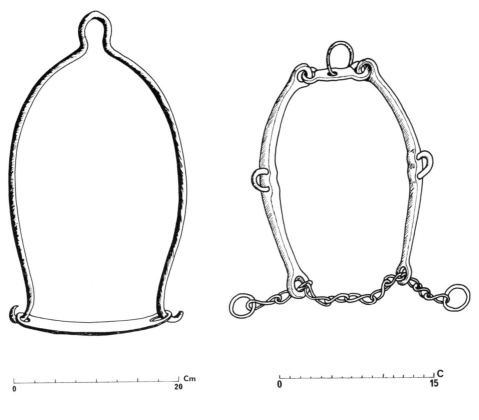

61 An iron *bowsell*.

62 Iron *branks*.

When wheeling the *neep-barra* or the *muck-barra* along the byre, it was said to be 'teen ben 'e greep', though strictly speaking it was going along the passage between the two *greeps*, since cattle were stalled at each side.

The farm had two byres. The one first entered off the *neep-shed* was the *coo-byre* for the *kye*, and beyond and in line with it was the *feeder's byre*, for *quaiks* and *stots* being fattened for eventual sale. The collective term for the cattle beasts was *the nowt*. The *coo-byre* had seven double stalls and three small single ones for young beasts. One double stall was enclosed to make a loose box for three calves. The feeders' byre had 8 double stalls. The door at its end opened into the barn, again with a vertically sliding door, and from

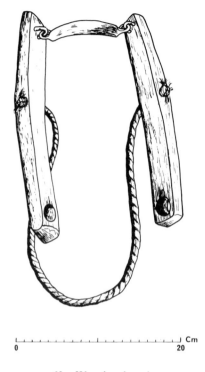

63   Wooden *branks*.

here the straw for feeding and bedding was carried in fork loads. All told, a total of 33 *nowt* and three or more calves (called *calfies*; the older plural, *caar*, though known, had gone out of use) could be kept if the farm was stocked to the full, though this did not normally happen.

The cows had their own 'personal' names or descriptions, as a *Diary* (1938) tells: '18 January, Peggie calved; 3 April, Janet cow calved; 17 November, 'blue heifer' calved; 2 December, Peggie calved again.

The farm had no bull, and in the days before artificial insemination, the cows had to be taken to the bull at a neighbouring farm when they 'startit rinnin''. In that case, the cow's face was fitted with *branks*, a kind of bridle or halter of iron and a chain, or rope or leather strap, of such a form that if the cow jerked at the tether, the *branks* tightened and it squeezed its own nose. The *Diary* for 1929 records, 'I got a branx from Alick Shand' (21 March).

If the *bullin'* went well, a calf followed in due course. The 1929 story, which flows on from 1928, was:

1928	
28 Nov	'Peggie calved.'
1929	
2 Jan	'Peggie cow at Pitglassie forenoon and Rosie calved in the evening.'
16 Feb	'our young blue cow was in calving evening, calved about one o'clock twin calves the first one of only lived a few minutes.' (She was a 5-year-old.)
21 Apr	'Willie was at Pitglassie with Rosie cow.'
12 June	'Willie gathering weeds and then went to Pitglassie with blue cow.'
25 June	'Jim and me up at Pitglassie with Janet cow.' (This was a 3-year-old that had come from Wartle. She had last calved on 11 December 1928).

Bill Wilson at Mid Pitglassie had the Board of Agriculture bull. Jimmy Chalmers at Pitglassie had it before that, and Jimmy Cooper, Auldyoch, had it for a while. More recently a Hereford bull kept by Peter Cowie, Uppermill, was used to serve cows.

64   Central Auction Mart, Turriff.

At one time, animals were sometimes tethered outside, for example calves out for the first time that needed to be tamed down a bit. For this, an iron *baikie* or tether stake, about a foot long, was hammered into the ground. It had an iron loop at the top, and the animal was fixed to the loop by means of a chain or rope with a swivel.

Coggit calfies were calves at the stage of taking milk from a *cog* or pail, as opposed to a *sookin' calfie*, which still sucked the cow. A cow suckling calves was a *sooker*. A *stot* was a male calf that had been castrated or *libbit*. A *heifer* was a female calf, and a *quaik*, *queyock* or *quaikie* one that was capable of being in calf. *Stirks* was more of a collective term, used after the calves had reached the stage of being *spent*, ie no longer dependent on their mother's milk.

Stirks were sold at three years old, being taken by the contractor, Wilson of Findon, to the Central Auction Mart in a *float*. There were two *marts* in Turriff at one time, but the second, Johnston & Paterson's, was eventually bought out by Central.

There were recognised experts in the area who saw to the castrating of calves with their *libbin-knives*. One was George Mintie. 'He roupit oot o' Mains o' Tollo, syne geed intae Brownside o' Montblairy. Aifter 'e retiret 'e hid a hoose in Turra an' cam up fae there tae dee 'e job.' When he stopped, Ackie Gray from Hill of Hatton did it. He and his father before him had included this in the range of jobs they did. The vet from Turriff might also do the job. *Diary* entries for 1923 are: 'Mr Forrest VS called forenoon and cut the calfie' (2 July), 'Geo Minty casterate the Paddie calfie' (6 December).

THE PLOO

Ploughing with horses took up much more of the year before the tractor came. It went on from January till April and then from October till December. In 1937, it took 77 days or parts of days, not always in good conditions. The *Diary* entry for 26 March is 'plowin in bad order', and work went on also on 25 December, 'a green Christmas'.

It took a good deal of skill to be a good ploughman, and some planning and preparation was needed before entry to a field with a plough. The first step was to take a spade and set up a line of sods, *props*, along the line of the old *midses*, where two *rigs* had come together. The *mids* marked the line of the dividing furrow or rather pair of furrows, one turned to the right and one to the left, so that a hollow remained in the field. Later working of the ground helped to fill this in, and the filling in of *midses* with the plough was a job to be done when preparing the ground for the coming crops. The number of rows of *props* set up depended on the state of the ground. They helped to guide the ploughman and let him divide the field tidily into the right number of *rigs*.

For those who pined for greater precision, *feerin-poles* about 3 or 4 feet high were sometimes stuck in the ground, but though Mr Hunter spoke of them, he had never seen them used. In the special case of ploughing matches, actual lines were laid along the ground to avoid as far as possible all risks of 'ga'n aff 'e stracht'.

When the *props* had been set up, the first stage in ploughing began. This was 'tae ca' tae the props', when a shallow *scrat* was made and not a *fur* of full depth. The first pair of *scrats*, one up and one down, was at a depth of about 1½ in or a little more, leaving 'just a little rimmie turned ower'. The two slices turned by making these *scrats* came against each other in a shallow, inverted V-shape. The next two *furs* were then ploughed up and down, the point of entry being about 6 in away from the *scrats*, but still not all at the full ploughing depth, which was reached only after 4 or 5 furrows had been ploughed. In technical terms, if the ridge-centres are seen as positives and the *midses* as negatives, then a line across the field at right-angles to the ploughing would appear as a slow-moving wave pattern of positive highs and negative lows.

The whole operation of reaching the proper ploughing depth was called *feerin'*, a word which means more than simply the cutting of the first furrow in a field. Real art was shown in keeping the *feerin* level with the rest of the ploughing. It refers, therefore, to the set of six, eight or ten furrows at the centre of a *rig*, even though these are invisible if the ploughing is well done.

When *feered*, the ploughman continued to plough his rig, up one side, down the other. At ploughing matches, a quarter of an acre was reckoned as a *rig* for competition purposes. At each end he turned his plough and team on the *eynrig*, also called the *heidrig* or *fleed*, a word which goes back to at least 1808 in Aberdeenshire. The *Diary* for 1923 notes on 27 January: 'ploughed endrigs of Stubble and filled in some midses', and on 15 March: 'filled in lea midses and ploughed endrigs'. *Siderigs* and *midrigs* are also mentioned.

A special cultivation technique described by Mr Hunter was *brak-furrin'*. For this, 'ye ebb-plooed aa 'e time, just deep eneuch tae turn a bittie ower in 'e aatumn, an' left it tae lie aa winter that wye, syne a gweed teer up in 'e spring wi' a harra or spring-tine, syne a gweed deep fur. Aa deen awa wi' lang syne. It gi'ed a fine tilth for neeps.' It was also done in weedy ground to help to kill the weeds. Another technique was *cross-plooin*, not much practised, but on some lands there was a regulation that if a tenant was going out, he had to cross-plough land already ploughed, and the incoming tenant had to put it into turnips. 'It wisna a gweed job cross-plooin, the yird widna come aff o' 'e cleathin.'

Since the nature of the ground could vary, the ploughman had to be able to make rapid adjustments as he went along, or else had to adjust the lie of the *sock* or coulter, or the place of linkage at the bridle. 'Tae gie 'e ploo mair yird' is to give the point of the plough a steeper pitch, so that it ploughed a little more deeply. The command to do this was, 'Haad 'er up ahin!' 'Tae gie 'e sock yird' is to bend down the tip of the sock, an operation which had to be done in the smiddy to make it dig in more. For lateral adjustments the plough would be given *mair lan'*, so that it cut a wider furrow slice.

The ploughman stood between the *stilts* of the plough, and was sometimes jocularly referred to as the *docknail*, the indispensable nail at, so to speak, the plough's posterior. Linking the stilts were *steys*. The mouldboard which turned the furrow slice to the right was the *cleathin'*. The flat side of the plough-body that moved next the unploughed land, in line with the vertical coulter, was the *lan' side*. Overlapping the sole that ran on the ground, and the front of the *breist o' the ploo* was the *sock*, which penetrated the soil horizontally and was so shaped that the furrow slice began its flow up and along it to the mould-board.

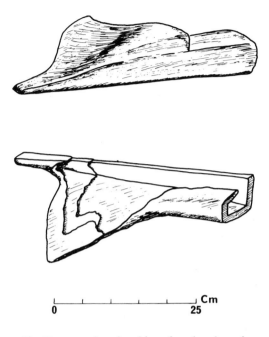

65 Upper and under sides of a plough sock.

The *sock* consisted of three elements: the *pint*, the *fedder* and the *barrel*. The feather was the flange that undercut the grassy roots as it passed through the soil. If new iron was added in the smiddy to the edge of a worn feather, or to a worn point, this was known as *layin' 'e sock*. There was a *feather lay*, and a *pint lay*. The coulter could also be laid in this way.

The method of fastening the coulter to the beam had a part to play in plough adjustment also. Older coulters had flat shanks that passed through an opening, or *box*, in the beam. They were held in place by four wedges, two wide ones at the sides, and two narrow ones at the end. By tightening or slackening one or more of these, the lie of the coulter could be slightly altered as required, or the tip could be raised and lowered. More recent coulters had round shanks and were fixed to the side of the beam by means of an iron *buckle* that straddled it. It was possible to turn such a coulter slightly to the left for the plough to be *gi'en mair lan'*, if necesary, or back, for less.

For the type with wedges, a *ploo-haimmer* was a necessity. 'Ye set 'e coulter first, syne tappit 'e wedges in. I've seen fyles 'e coulter fine set an'

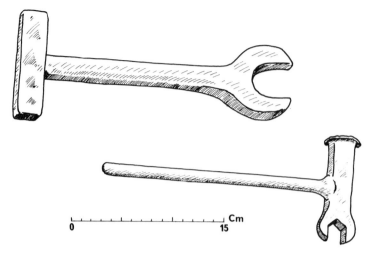

66   Two types of plough-hammer.

ye'd come yark against a steen—knockit 'e wedges a' oot.' The coulter was set so that the point should be about three finger breadths above the tip of the sock, or more in stony ground. It should be set very slightly into the land, which helped it to turn down the grass that was to be ploughed under.

The *ploo-haimmer* hung in an iron loop inside the body of the plough. One at Brownhill was said to have been the hammer of the second plough at the farm of Carlincraig in the time of Mr Hunter's father. Though its main purpose was to adjust the coulter, it was also sometimes used to hammer down the point of the *sock*, cold, when it was 'scarce o' yird', though this was not a good thing to do since the point was liable to break off altogether. This example had been used latterly for hammering *sharps* into horseshoes in frosty weather. *Sharps*, also called *pikes* or *cogs*, were fixed into *cog-holes* on the shoes. If cog-holes had to be made in new shoes, the process was called *frostin' 'e sheen,*so a cog-hole might also be called a *frost-hole*. *Frostin'* was done at the approach of winter.

For ploughing *ley*, a *cuttin' wheel* was buckled on to the forepart of the beam. According to Mr Hunter, 'Some fowk used wheels steady, bit fin I startit first we wisna alloo't tae use a wheel for stibble or clean lan'.' He started ploughing at 'Cyarlins' (Carlincraig), 'didna get muckle learnin'—pitt'n awa wi' a pair o' horses an' a ploo an' mak 'e best o't'. The *cuttin wheel*, which cut the firm turf in front of the coulter with its sharp disc-shaped blade, was regularly used in ploughing matches, however.

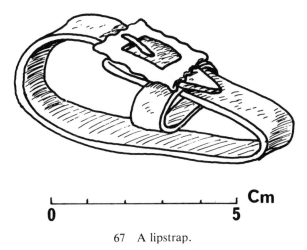

67   A lipstrap.

Another attachment was the *skreefer*, which replaced the coulter, in appearance like a mini-mouldboard. It turned the grass and muck well into the bottom of the furrow, and in fact, many modern tractor ploughs use a *skreefer* only, and no coulter.

As an extra refinement at ploughing matches, 'fyles they vrocht a cheyn wi' a ball on 'e eyn', which helped to flatten out unevennesses.

The front or muzzle of the plough-beam contained a number of openings set above each other. By fixing the pin of the bridle lower or higher, the plough could be adjusted for depth. The bridle itself was notched, and by fixing the *yoke* more to the right or more to the left, adjustment for *land* could be given.

The strong 5-ft long wooden yoke held the pair of 3-ft *swingletrees* by means of an iron hook and *hesp* at each end. From the ends of the swingletree, the *theets* ran forward, being supported by hooks on the *backbin* and continuing to the hooks in the *haims* that hugged the collar of each horse. The *backbin* was a broad, leather strap over the horse's back, having no particular function other than to keep the *theets* from falling among the horse's feet, and to support the reins.

As a point of sophistication, a very short swingletree, only 1 ft 6 in long, was put on when the last furrow was being ploughed close to a fence, since one of normal length would have caught on the *palin' posts*.

The horses that drew the plough often had their special positions, and were named accordingly. The one that was used to walking on the land-side or near-side was the *lanner*; the offside horse was the *furrer* or *fur-beast*. A *fur-beast* that tramped in the *fur* was no use at a ploughing match. Expressions used of horses with particular attributes were: 'A gran' lanner!, a gran' furrer!, a gran' aff-sider! tidy in 'e fur!'

Plough harness was simple, consisting of the collar and *haims*, the *backbin* that supported the theets, and the *rynes* which were attached to the rings of the bit and brought back through the metal loops of the *haims* and the leather loop of the *backbin*. The bridle on the horse's head consisted of the *broobin*, and two *lipstraps* which were fixed to the bit.

GLOSSARY

Aa   all
Aal   old
Ahin   behind
Aixle   axle

Baabee   halfpenny
Backbin   back band, in harness
Back-chain, -cheyn   chain over saddle to support cart shafts
Back door   tail board of cart
Backet   handled, scoop-like box for lifting grain, turnips etc
Badder   bother
Bag-raip   rope around eaves of stack
Baikie   tether-peg
Bailie, bylie   to look after cattle, cattleman
Bairn   child
Ban'ster   one who binds sheaves
Belly-ban'   belly-band, in harness
Bere   4- or 6-rowed barley
Big   to build
Bigger   builder
Bile   boil
Bink   ledge at side of fire
Binnin   binding for fastening cattle
Bishop   device for firming loosened soil; to firm loosened soil
Blin' bridle   bridle with blinkers
Blin' sieve   sieve with solid base
Blin' tit   blind teat
Blon'e   'blonde', girl friend
Bobbin John   turnip seed sowing device
Bone Davy   manure sowing machine
Boortree   elder tree
Bothy   room for single farm servants looking after themselves
Bout   line of shearing
Bow   boll
Bowsell   iron cattle-binding
Bowster   bolster

Brak-fur   to plough shallow furrows
Brander   open metal frame for baking scones or roasting fish over a fire
Branks   halter of wood or iron
Breer   to shoot, of crops
Breid   oatcakes
Britchin   breeching
Broadcast   broadcast sowing machine
Broobin   brow band (harness)
Brooky   sooty, nickname for blacksmith
Brose   oatmeal dish made by pouring boiling water on meal
Brose-caup   wooden bowl for brose
Bruise-box   a *cornkist*
Bull   to serve a cow
Bum-bee   bumble bee
Buncher   machine attached to mill for making straw bunches
Bushle, bussle   bushel measure
Butt   tail of sheaf
Bylie   see *Bailie*
Byre   cow shed

Carr   calves
Caff   chaff
Calfie's cheese   beestings
Cassied   cobbled
Catcher   town-keeper at week-ends
Caup   wooden bowl
Chaamer   room for single farm-servants getting meals in kitchen
Chackie   linen bag for carrying dirty washing
Charge   oath
Chessel, chesset   cheese-vat
Clapper   butter hand
Clean lan'   land after a root crop
Cleathin   mould-board
Cloo   ball of coiled rope
Close   farmyard
Clyack   end of cutting harvest
Clyack shafe   the last sheaf to be cut
Cog   (a) frost-nail (b) wooden pail; to put a calf on to feeding from a pail
Coggit calf   a calf no longer sucking but still getting milk
Cole   hay cock
Coo-byre   cowshed
Corn -laft, -kist, -yard   oats, grain-loft, corn-chest, stackyard
Cornkister   farm-workers' song, 'bothy ballad'

Cottar -man   married farm-servant living in a tied *cottar-hoose*
Cowp   empty, tip up
Crap   to put in crop
Crude-brakker   curd-breaker
Crudes   curds
Crusie   double-shelled oil-lamp
Cuffins   fragments of straw
Cut   castrate
Cyacks   oatcakes

Deem   'dame' kitchen-maid
De'il   devil
Dist   'dust' particles of meal and husk
Docken   dock
Docknail   mainpin
Doocot   dovecot
Dreel   drill
Dwine   pine

Easin' gyang   row of sheaves at the eaves of a stack
Easin's   eaves
Eave raip   rope around eaves of a stack
Ebb-ploo   to shallow plough
Edder   to rope thatch with an *edderin*
Edderin   shuttle shaped ball of rope
E'e   eye
Eemist wynin'   upper part of field
Eeran   errand
Eest   used
Eident   busy
Ether   udder
Eynrig   end ridge

Faar   where
Fan, fanner   winnowing machine
Fan, fin   when
Fedder   feather
Fee   to hire a farm-hand
Feeder   a cattle-beast being fattened
Feer   to set up the first furrow in ploughing a field
Feerin   group of first furrows
Feerin pole   pole used as marker in setting up the first furrow
Fee't man   hired hand

Fess   fetch
Fillies   felloes of wheel
Fit   what
Fite   white
Flannen   flannel
Fleed, eynrig   end ridge
Float   lorry for carrying livestock
Foo   how
Foon   foundation
Fore slings   for attaching harness at front of cart shaft
Forestaa   front stall
Forrit   forward
Front shelvin'   movable board on front of box-cart
Frost   to fit frost nails
Frost-hole   frost nail hole
Funs   whins, gorse
Fur   furrow
Fur-beast   horse for walking in furrow
Furrer   horse walking in furrow
Fye   whey
Fyles   whiles, sometimes

Gad   'goad' wand
Gaither   to gather, of butter
Gaitherer   one who gathers grain to make sheaves
Gang   go
Garron-nails   retaining pins through floor and axle of box cart
Gavel   tail of sheaf
Girnel   meal, storage box
Girse hyeuk, grass hyeuk   metal strut on scythe
Gowpenfae   double handful
Graip   four-pronged fork
Greep   byre-drain
Grieve   farm overseer
Grubber   heavy iron 'harrow' with cultivator tyres
Gudge   gudgeon, pin
Guiser   young disguised caller exchanging entertainment for gifts
Gyang   row

Haal   haul, pull
Haim   curved piece of wood or metal on horse collar
Hairst   harvest
Hale   whole

Halflin   young farm-servant
Hangie   hangman, a soft cheese
Happer   hopper
Heck   slatted frame for straw or hay in byre
Heedin' shafe   the last sheaf on top of a stack
Heid rig   head ridge
Heid-stall   'head-stall', part of halter
Heifer   female calf
Helter   halter
Hert   to fill the heart of a stack or cart-load of grain
Hesp   hasp
Hey -cole, -laft, -ruck   hay -cock, -loft, -stack
Hin' shelvin   movable board on *back door* of box cart
Hin' slings   part of britchin, for attachment to rear of cart shaft
Hogmanay   New Year's Eve
Howk   dig
Hyeuk   sickle
Hyow   hoe

Ill-gruntit   cantankerous
Ily lamp   'oil' lamp, *crusie*

Kebbick, kibbick   a cheese
Kirn   churn
Kist   chest
Knot girse   knot grass
Knotty tams   a dish of boiled milk with meal cast in
Kye   cows

Laich   low
Laid   flattened, of a crop
Lanner   land-side horse
Lan'side   the side of the plough next to the unploughed land
Lame   earthenware
Latter-oot   'letter out', the one who feeds in the straw in rope twisting
Lay   to put more iron on a sock or coulter
Lead   to cart home grain etc.
Ley   lea
Lib   castrate
Lifter   one who gathers grain to make sheaves
Lippie   measure for bruise for feeding horse
Loon   boy, lad
Loo-warm   lukewarm
Lowse   loosen, untie

Lowser   one who cuts bands on sheaves during threshing
Lyin-shafts   main beams under box cart

Maamie   thick, mellow, of broth
Mait   food
Mart   market
Mell   mallet, heavy hammer
Midrig   mid ridge
Mids   division between two ridges
Midden   dunghill
Milk-broth   a dish made with milk and barley
Milkin' steel   milking stool
Mull   mill
Muck-barra   manure barrow
Murl   crumble
Murly tuck   dish of oatcakes crumbled into milk

Naithmist wynin   lower part of field
Neep   turnip
Neep-barra   turnip barrow
Neep-click   tool for pulling turnips
Neep-corn   an oat crop following turnips
Neeperin'   neighbouring
Neep hasher   turnip slicer
Neep-pluck   tool for pulling turnips
Neep-reet   land cleared of turnips for a following grain crop
Neesht, neest   next
Notice   to take heed of, by giving something
Nowt   cattle

Orra-man   wire tightening lever, in fencing
Orra-loon   young farm servant
Oxter-stav'   'armpit stave', crutch

Pace   Easter
Palin'   fence
Park   field
Pat   small ball of butter
Patcher   turnip seed sowing device
Peer-man   wire-tightening lever, in fencing
Picker   lever for removing staples
Piece   snack
Pig   pot, jar
Pike   frost-nail

Pinch   crowbar used in fencing
Piz-meal, pizzers   pease-meal
Plot   scald
Plump-churn   plunge churn
Plumper   plunger of pump churn
Potestatur   prime
Pottitch   porridge
Prop   ploughing marker
Pu'   pull
Pun'   pound
Pykit weer   barbed wire

Quaick, quaickie, queyock   young female cattle beast
Quarterer   a tramp getting quarters in the steading and doing some farm work

Raff up   bulk up
Raip   rope
Rakin's   gathering of loose hay
Rash   rush
Ream   ream
Redd roads   clear paths round a crop for a binder
Reest   roost
Restin' pole   movable pole under cart-shaft to take weight during rests
Rig   ridge
Rin   'run', be in heat, of a cow
Risp   rasp
Rodden   rowan
Roup   sale
Ruck   stack
Ruck-ledder   stack ladder
Runch   wild radish
Rynes   reins

Saach   willow
Saiddle   saddle
Scrat   shallow furrow
Scythe-brod   sharpening board for scythe
Search   milk strainer
Seck-lifter   hand-barrow
Sell   cattle binding
Setting by   laying near at hand
Shaa   shaw
Shaave, shaaver   to sow, sower
Shafe -fork, -eyn   sheaf, -fork, -end

Shafter, shaftit weskit   sleeved waistcoat
Shakker   shaker in a mill
Shalt   mill horse
Shalt-loon   young farm servant looking after the *shalt*
Sharp   frost-nail
Sheelicks   light grains of corn
Sheen   shoes
Shelvin'   movable board on box-cart
Shim   horse-hoe
Short dung   well rotted dung
Siderig   side ridge
Side-shelvin'   movable board on side of box-cart
Sids   'seeds' particles of oat-bran
Siftin' riddle   riddle for small seed
Siller   'silver', money
Single   hoe turnips
Sinker   weight for fastening horse in stall
Skellach   charlock or wild mustard
Skimmer   pan for skimming cream
Skiry   gaudy
Skreefer   skimmer for surface soil and weeds
Slider   (a) retaining rod for cattle binding; (b) harness fitment on cart shaft
Sloack   quench thirst
Snap an' rattle   dish of oatcakes crumbled into milk, *murly-tuck*
Sned   scythe handle
Sock   plough share
Soo   rectangular stack
Sooker   cow suckling calves
Sookin' calfie   a sucking calf
Souter   shoemaker
Sowens   flummery, made from *sids*
Spen'   to wean
Sprots   reedy plants
Spurkle   wooden stirring rod
Staa   stall, floor of stall
Stame mull   steam mill
Stame-mull breid   thick, poorly-made oatcakes
Steer   stir
Steilert   'steelyard', weighing machine
Stibble   stubble
Stilt   handle of plough
Stirk   young cattle beast past the stage of getting milk
Stook   shock of grain
Stot   young castrated male cattle beast

Straik (a) sharpening board or stone for scythe;
        (b) wooden cylinder for levelling a bushel measure
Strainer, strainin' post posts taking the strain of the wire in fencing
Strae straw
Strake 'stroke', in harrowing
Strang urine
Strapper young farm servant looking after the *shalt*
Sup, suppie small quantity
Swad Swedish turnip
Swap to rope thatch with a *cloo*
Sweevle swivel
Sye to filter milk, a milk strainer
Syer milk strainer
Syne then

Tailer tool for taking roots off turnips
Taings 'tongs', hinged wire-tightener in fencing
Tansy ragwort
Tapner tool for taking tops off turnips
Tattie, -corn potato, -corn
Thack, theek thatch
Theet trace-chain or -rope
Thoom-piece oatcakes buttered with thumb, as a snack
Thoom raip thumb rope
Thorther, thorter to cross harrow
Thraa-crook, -hyeuk ropetwister
Thrammle, trammle chain on cattle binding
Thristle thistle
Throat-lash part of a halter
Tillie-pan metal pan used as a scoop
Tit teat
Toon farm town
Toondie town-keeper at week-ends
Tow twine
Tramp-cole a large hay cock, made up of smaller ones
Tramp pick crowbar with foot step, for levering out posts
Trevis stall partition
Troch trough
Trock(s) odds and ends
Tummlin-tam hay gatherer
Turned gyang row of sheaves on a stack, with the shear underneath
Tweezler, tweezlick ropetwister
Twiner ropetwister

Umman   woman

Vrocht   worked

Wecht   (a) weight; (b) a *blin' sieve*, 'sieve' with a solid base
Weety   rather wet
Wheeber   whistling sound
Win   to dry
Winlin   bunch of straw
Winnister   winnowing machine
Winraa   windrow, gathered row of hay
Winter, to get   to clear the fields of harvested grain
Wynin   division of a field

Yalla   yellow turnip
Yark   jerk
Yarr   corn-spurrey
Yavel   second year oats
Yird   earth
Yirnin   rennet